OARED
FIGHTING SHIPS

Frontispiece: The Victory of Samothrace. Louvre, Paris

Oared
Fighting Ships

*From Classical times to the
coming of steam*

By R. C. ANDERSON, Litt. D.

Model and Allied Publications

ARGUS BOOKS LTD.

*First published 1962
New edition 1976*

ISBN 0 85242 471 X

*Printed and bound in Great Britain by Morrison & Gibb Ltd, London and Edinburgh,
for the publishers, Argus Books Ltd, Station Road, Kings Langley, Herts.*

Introduction

The birthplace of the galley, the fighting ship propelled by oars, was somewhere in the eastern Mediterranean, possibly in Crete. It was not on the Nile, as anthropologists of the 'everything from Egypt' school would like us to believe, for there is no evidence that Egypt produced anything that could possibly be called a galley until long after such craft were well established in Greece and the Greek colonies. The change from paddles to oars may have been made first by the Egyptians, but it was left for the peoples of the Aegean to develop the mere rowing-boat into a man-of-war.

Once introduced, the type proved remarkably persistent, even when faced by competition from the far later sailing man-of-war. There were fighting galleys in the Levant from Homeric times or very little later until the end of the 18th century A.D., a matter of at least 2,500 years; while in the Baltic oared men-of-war lasted even later, and were only rendered obsolete by the coming of steam.

The story of the oared fighting ship is thus much longer than that of its sailing rival. Until cannon had become something more than a mere substitute for bows or slings there was nothing to distinguish the man-of-war of northern seas from any other large sailing ship; whereas in the Mediterranean the 'long ship' meant for fighting had been sharply differentiated from the 'round ship' of commerce for 2,000 years or more.

It was also far more varied. From its first appearance in the 15th century to its death at the hands of the steam engine in the 19th the sailing man-of-war changed very little except for a series of small improvements here and there and a steady increase in dimensions; but the Mediterranean galley, with a life more than fives times as long, underwent many drastic changes of design and many ups-and-downs in size before it returned on its death-bed to a form very like that of its ancestor of 2,500 years before.

This makes it difficult to trace the story of its development as a straightforward self-contained whole; so difficult that I have not attempted to do so, but have covered it – as far as I could – in six studies, each devoted to a comparatively short period. To these I have added a chapter on the galeass, a large Mediterranean type with something of the sailing ship in her ancestry, and then, leaving the Mediterranean, I have dealt with the English galleys (so called) of the reign of Edward I, the galeasses, pinnaces and rowbarges of Henry VIII, and some ill-defined hybrids of the 17th and 18th centuries, mainly English. Finally I have described the strange rowing vessels produced in the Baltic just as the life of the Mediterranean galley was approaching its undistinguished end.

Parts of the earlier chapters are frankly argumentative, but since argument on these subjects has been going on for more than 500 years without leading to agreement, this is understandable. The evidence available is too scanty and too contradictory for anything to be proved beyond doubt; a verdict can only be a matter of personal assessment of probability. In such cases I have tried to present the case for conclusions already reached in my own mind, hoping to convince others that these conclusions are justified.

The choice of illustrations has been difficult. For some periods 'pictorial' evidence is almost non-existent, for others it is embarrassingly plentiful. The English 'galleys' of about A.D. 1300 have had to remain unrepresented save for my own purely conjectural drawing and the dromons of the Eastern Roman Empire are in little better case, while easily available representations of Mediterranean galleys of the 17th and 18th centuries must run into hundreds. Portraits of early Greek galleys are also plentiful, but usually so crude and so difficult to understand that I have hesitated to include them. They may be found in profusion in Moll's *Das Schiff in der bildenden Kunst*, a collection covering the history of the ship, as seen by artists, from the earliest times to the end of the Middle Ages.

The Greek trireme appeared in the hey-day of Greek art, but unfortunately ships have seldom proved good subjects for sculpture and although a good number of representations of galleys of the classical period have been preserved they are all sufficiently vague to leave room for widely differing interpretations. Some of these have been reproduced again and again, but it has been necessary to include them for the sake of arguing about them. For later periods I have tried to avoid some of the more hackneyed pictures and drawings in favour of those of my own choice. No doubt others would have chosen differently and would probably have relied less on models, but I hope my selection will at least be acceptable as illustrating the text with which it appears.

Contents

List of Plates

Unless otherwise noted the photographs have been supplied officially by the Museums concerned.

Nos. 23B to 25B are from contemporary models in the *Sjöhistoriska Museum, Stockholm*

List of Figures

Most of these figures have been redrawn by Mr. B. Landström, author of *The Ship* (1961), from my own pencil sketches. I am most grateful to him and to Prof. L. Casson, author of *The Ancient Mariners* (1959), who found for me some photographs illustrating Chapter 4.

Bibliography for Chapters I-IV

The following list of books and papers is by no means exhaustive. It omits a number of books written in Latin and printed during the 16th and 17th centuries and it makes no attempt to include the less important short articles in various periodicals. With these added the list might well be twice its present length.

The earlier books have their interest as literary curiosities, but are of very little help otherwise. The same might be said of some comparatively recent productions, but all in this list are at least worth examination, even if some of the theories set forth are obviously absurd.

Some of the books and articles listed are known to me only from references given by others, in particular by Luebeck and Marstrand (see below). For references to periodicals I have to thank Mr H. Szymanski, whose manuscript list has been extremely useful.

Where no place of publication is given this may be taken to be London and occasionally New York as well.

ALEXANDERSON *De Grekiska Trieren* — —, Lund, 1914.

ANDERSON *The Sailing Ship*, 1926 (1948). See also *The Mariner's Mirror*, 1914, 1933, 1934, 1941.

ASSMANN *Seewesen* (in Baumeister, *Denkmäler des klassischen Altertums*, Munich, 1887. Also many articles and reviews in German periodicals.

BAUER *Die Kriegsschiffe der Griechen*, Munich, 1890. Criticism of Kopecky and Assmann in *Neue Philologische Rundschau*, 1890.

BOECK *Urkunden über das Seewesen des attischen Staates*, Berlin, 1840.

BREUSING *Die Nautik der Alten*, Bremen, 1886.
Die Lösung des Trierenrätsels, Bremen, 1889.

BUSLEY *Die Entwicklung des Segelschiffes* — —, Berlin, 1920.

CARLI-RUBBI *Delle Trireme* (in *Opere*, IX), Milan, 1785.

CARLINI *Les Galères antiques* (in *Bulletin de l'Association technique maritime et aéronautique*, 1934).

CARTAULT *La Trière athénienne* — —, Paris, 1881.

CASSON — *The Ancient Mariners*, 1959.

COOK AND RICHARDSON — *Triremes* (in *The Mid-Tyne Link*, 1906).

CYBULSKI — *Die griechischen und römischen Schiffe*, Leipzig, 1900.

DE LA GRAVIÈRE — *La Marine des Anciens*, Paris, 1890.

DESLANDES — *Essai sur la Marine des Anciens — —*, Paris, 1768.

DOLLEY — *The Warships of the later Roman Empire* (in *Journal of Roman Studies*, 1948).

DROYSEN — *Die griechische Kriegsschiffe* (in *Heerwesen der Griechen*, Freiburg, 1889).

DUFOUR — *Mémoire sur les Vaisseaux de Guerre des Anciens*, Geneva, 1842.

EINS — *Das Rudern bei den Alten*, Danzig, 1896.

GARRETT — *On Ancient Galleys* (in *Dublin Quarterly Journal*, 1864).

GLOTIN — *Essai sur les Navires à Rangs de Rames des Anciens*, Paris, 1862.

GRASER — *De Veterun Re Navali*, Berlin, 1864.
Das Trierenrelief der Akropolis (in *Berliner archäologische Zeitung*, 1864).
Das Model eines athenischen Funfreihenschiffes — —, Berlin, 1866 (1873).
Untersuchungen über das Seewesen des Alterthums, Göttingen, 1870.

HAACK — *Über attische Trieren* (in *Zeitschrift des Vereines deutscher Ingenieure*, 1895).

HOLMES — *Ancient and Modern Ships*, Part I, 1900.

HOWELL — *An Essay on the War-Galleys of the Ancients*, Edinburgh, 1826.

JAL — *Archéologie navale*, Paris, 1840.
La Flotte de César, Paris, 1861.

KOPECKY — *Die attischen Trieren*, Leipzig, 1890.

LAIRD CLOWES — *Sailing Ships — —*, Part I, 1930.

LAMPE — *Die athenische Kriegstriere* (in *Wassersport*, Berlin, 1884).

LEMAITRE — *De la Disposition des Rameurs sur la Trière antique* (in *Revue Archéologique*, Paris, 1883).

LE ROY — *La Marine des anciens Peuples — —*, Paris, 1777.
Les Navires des Anciens — —, Paris, 1883.
Nouvelles Recherches sur le Vaisseau long des Anciens, Paris, 1786.
Des Navires employés par les Anciens — —, Paris, 1802–3.

LINDSAY — *History of Merchant Shipping* (Vol. 1), 1874.

MARKS — *Nero's great Canal, with some Remarks on Roman War Galleys* (in *Transactions of the Royal Society of Literature*, 1900).

MARSTRAND   *Arsenalet i Piraeus* — —, Copenhagen, 1922.

MELVILLE   *On the Rowers in Ancient Galleys* (in Pownall, *Treatise on the Study of Antiquities* — —, 1782).

MOLL   *Das Schiff in der bildenden Kunst*, Berlin, 1929.

MONTFAUCON   *Recherches* — — *sur* — — *la Construction des Navires des Anciens*, Paris, 1747.

MORRISON   *The Greek Trireme* (in *The Mariner's Mirror*, 1941).

NEWMAN   *Ancient Sea Galleys* — — (in *Transactions of the Royal Society of Literature*, 1915).

RODGERS   *Greek and Roman Naval Warfare*, Annapolis, 1937.
Naval Warfare under Oars, Annapolis, 1939.

RONDOLET   *Mémoire sur la Marine des Anciens* — —, Paris, 1820.

SCHMIDT   *Berichte über das Seewesen im Altertum* (in *Jahresberichte für klassischen Altertumswissenschaft*, 1892 and 1897).
Über griechische Dreireiher, Berlin, 1899.

SERRE   *La Trière athenienne* (in *Mémoires* — — *Academie des Sciences*, Paris, 1884).

SMITH   *The Voyage of St Paul* — — *and the Ships of the Ancients*, 1848.

SOTTAS   *Les Caracteristiques de la Triere atténienne* (in *Academie de Marine*, 1922).

STAHLECKER   *Über die verschiedenen Versuche der Rekonstruktion der attischen Triere*, Ravensburg, 1897.

TARN   *The Greek Warship* (in *Journal of Hellenic Studies*, 1905).
Hellenistic Military and Naval Developments, Cambridge, 1930.
The Oarage of Greek Warships (in *The Mariner's Mirror*, 1933). Also Notes in this volume and the next.

TENNE   *Kriegsschiffe* — — *der* — — *Griechen und Römer*, Oldenburg, 1916.

TORR   *Ancient Ships*, Cambridge, 1894.
Navis (in Daremberg and Saglio, *Dictionnaire des Antiquités* — —. Paris, 1904).

VOIGT   *Der Schiffsbug von Samothrake* — — (in *Schiffbau*, 1912). Also many short articles in periodicals.

WARRE   *Navis* (in Smith, *Dictionary of Greek and Roman Antiquities*, 3rd edn, 1891).

WILLIAMS   *Early Greek Ships of Two Levels* (in *Journal of Hellenic Studies*, 1958).

I

Galleys before the Trireme

It is very hard to define a galley with any precision. In this series of studies the word will be used to denote a vessel of moderate size intended for fighting under oars. Size must be considered, to distinguish galleys from smaller craft such as the gunboats of Napoleonic times and from the larger galeasses of the 17th century or the rowing frigates of the 18th; while at the same time the stipulation as to fighting has to be made, to exclude oared vessels used only for the transport of goods or passengers, or even of fighting men, if their fighting was to be done ashore rather than afloat.

A second point to be decided is at what stage in ancient history or pre-history the large open rowing boat became a galley. This is easier, because we have only to consider how a galley fought before the introduction of cannon; to qualify as a galley the vessel must have a ram-bow. The test is a crude one and we shall find certain important exceptions, but it must serve for want of anything better.

Egyptian monuments suggest that the use of oars as opposed to paddles – a decisive step – began on the Nile somewhere about 3000 B.C. Our earliest knowledge of sea-going ships goes back to much the same date and comes from Crete, but is so slight that it hardly deserves to be called knowledge, for representations of Cretan ships are so small and so vague that they are almost useless as evidence. Some do seem to show ram-bows, but in many cases there is not even agreement as to which end is the bow and which the stern.

Homer, whether a single man or a syndicate, composing the Iliad between 900 and 800 B.C. and basing it on traditional accounts of events of about 1200, makes no mention of fighting at sea. His only use for ships in wartime is to carry fighting men from one country to attack another; even his pirates would be better called 'sea-raiders', since they found their booty ashore, as the Vikings did later.

In spite of this we know that a regular sea-battle – not by any means necessarily the first – was fought between Egyptians and 'peoples of the north' at about the same time as the siege of Troy, probably in 1194 B.C. Whether the Egyptian ships shown on the monument commemorating this battle can be considered galleys in the sense postulated above is a matter of controversy. They have oars and they have their bows finished off by heavy carved heads, but these are set at such an angle and carried so high above the water that they would be quite useless as rams; while the number of oars shown would not give sufficient speed to make even a well placed ram at all effective. What is certain is that the ships of the 'northerners,' probably from Syria or Asia Minor, have no sign of rams in any form or position.

There can, however, be no doubt that the ram was well established in the Levant by 800 B.C. or very little later. It appears on galleys depicted on Greek pottery of that period almost as clearly as on the Phoenician ships in Assyrian sculptures of about 700 and is shown in a form clearly meant for business, not as a mere survival of a projecting keel-plank. Ships with rams such as these must have been designed for warlike use and they are far too well developed for complete novelties. It is hard to believe that Homer knew nothing of such ships and their use. Possibly he looked on naval warfare as ungentlemanly and therefore not to be mentioned in connection with his 'god-like' heroes.

Homer's larger ships carried 52 men or in some cases 120. We know that the standard fighting ship just before the introduction of the trireme was the *pentekonter* of 50 oars and it seems reasonable to suppose that ships with crews of 52 men were of that class, there being 50 rowers, a helmsman and a 'boatswain of the oars,' the *keleustes* or time-beater. Ships of 120 men are not so easy to explain. Torr considered that they had 118 oars and had been derived from 60-oared craft by adding 58 oars at a different level in the spaces between the original 60 and so producing a bireme. The difficulty, to his mind, lay in the fact that 'the Greeks never employed 60-oared ships and apparently never knew that such existed, for they had no name for them.'[1] Believing, as he did, that all ancient galleys were rowed on the principle of one man to one oar he failed to see that a much simpler explanation would be to enlarge the vessel very slightly and let each oar be worked by two men.

In the same connection Tarn insisted that 'no bireme is ever heard of in the Greek world from the beginning of written records down to the Roman Empire – the name for it, *dieres*, is only a

[1] *Ancient Ships* (1894), p. 3.

dictionary word.'[1] This may be true, but it can hardly be denied that vessels did exist with oars arranged in such a way that they are best described by the Anglo-Latin word 'bireme,' if we are not to be allowed the Greek *dieres*. The Phoenician ships already mentioned and several of the Greeks agree in showing oars in two staggered rows with the vertical distance between these something like two-fifths of the distance between adjacent oars in the same row (Plates IA and IB). Most people would have no hesitation in calling these galleys 'biremes.'

Even if there were no pictorial evidence for biremes, we should be almost compelled to assume the existence of something of the sort, if only for a short time, to provide a link between the simple *pentekonter* and the very elaborate trireme. All the conflicting theories as to the arrangement of a trireme's oars agree on one thing, that in it three oars, or at least three rowers, were somehow fitted into a length of side hardly greater than that needed for a single oar on the earlier system. It is almost inconceivable that so drastic a change could have been made in a single step.

In actual fact we find the intermediate stage well shown on both monuments and pottery, two rows of oars with those of the lower row appearing about mid-way between those of the upper and, as far as can be estimated, some 15 or 18 in. lower down. Naturally the oars of the lower row were the shorter and their rowers sat nearer the vessel's side. The diagrams (Fig. 1) show how this could be done with oars of 9 ft and 14 ft, but it must be admitted that it is not easy to devise a satisfactory support for the seats of the upper rowers. Such evidence as there is seems to show that they did not row standing.

At this point a question arises. In developing the bireme from the original 'unireme' did ancient naval architects add the second row of oars above or below the first? Did they build up above the former gunwale or did they cut oar-ports below it? Practical experience would soon have led to the same result in either case, but the answer, if we knew it, would have its importance as an indication of the probable freeboard of a *pentekonter*. Xerxes used both triremes and *pentekonters* for his floating bridge across the Hellespont and it has been claimed that this proves that a trireme was too low in the water for any possibility of superposed banks of oars. The weak point in this reasoning is that there is nothing to show that ships of the two types were mixed; a long section of the bridge might well have been higher or lower than the rest without causing much inconvenience.

---

[1] *The Mariner's Mirror*, 1933, p. 60.

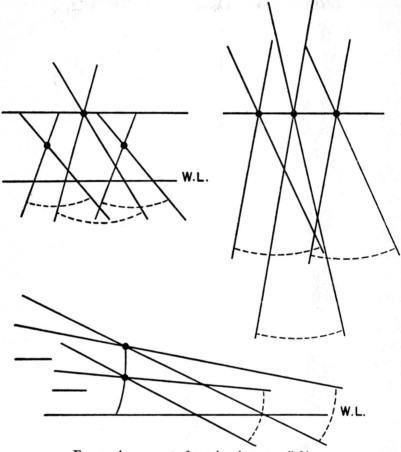

FIG. 1. *Arrangement of oars in a 'superposed' bireme*

If anything, the argument works the other way round. The next chapter will show that we are almost compelled to accept superposed oars in a trireme, and if a *pentekonter* had the same freeboard, it too would be capable of carrying oars at two levels. The suggestion runs contrary to the view usually taken, but it seems at the very least a possibility that in the days just before the introduction of the trireme there were *pentekonters* with their oars arranged in that way. Good representations of undoubted biremes show a number of oars ranging from 16 to 23 on one side and we shall see later that there is good reason to believe that *triakonters* or 30-oared galleys of later date also had oars at two levels. If it was found desirable to dispose as few as 15 oars in this apparently unnecessarily complicated manner, it would surely be even more so in the case of 25.

Unfortunately, if the *pentekonter* of about 500 B.C. was indeed a bireme with 13 oars a side in the longer row, we are confronted by a sudden doubling, or rather more, of that number to the 27 of the shortest row in a trireme and thus an increase of nearly 100 per cent in the vessel's length. Such a jump would be quite as hard to accept as that from a single-banked *pentekonter* to a three-banked trireme.

Evidence for short biremes with about 20 oars a side has been shown to be plentiful; that for vessels of the same kind long enough to be the immediate predecessors of the trireme is scarcer and less convincing, but it does exist. A number of fragments of Greek pottery show galleys with a second line of rowers on what looks like a sort of flying deck above the first and one actually shows a complete galley with 20 rowers on the lower level and 19 on the upper.[1] These representations have been interpreted as attempts by the artists to show the rowers on both sides of the ship at once, but it is far more natural to suppose that they mean what they say and do in fact show ships with rowers at two levels. A comparison with another better drawn ship helps to confirm this idea, for there, although we only see rowers on the upper deck, there is no doubt that we see also the thole-pins for a second row of oars beneath them.

Together these last representations make it evident that there were biremes with at least 40 oars a side and from that to the 54 recorded for the two lowest banks of a trireme is not too long a step for our acceptance; for, after all, the first triremes of about 550 B.C. were very likely not so long as those known to us from records of 200 years later. If the largest Homeric ships were indeed worked by something approaching 58 oars a side, there was no step to be taken.

The conclusion is this: The first and simplest galleys were single-banked open boats fitted with rams and rowed by anything up to 50 oars. By 700 B.C. at the very latest a second bank of oars had been introduced. Some galleys on the new plan had as few as 30 oars, but others more closely related to the original *pentekonter* might perhaps have as many as 100 in two rows of 25 on either side. When once this stage had been reached, the two existing banks could be left as they were and a trireme could be produced by adding an outrigger, *parekseiresia* or *apostis* to carry the oars of a third bank, that of the so-called *thranites*. This was the decisive step which made the classical galley into an extremely complicated fighting machine. The step was long, but it was taken from a footing already firmly established.

[1] See Köster, *Das antike Seewesen* (1923), p. 21 and plates 19, 26–28; Moll, *Das Schiff in der bildenden Kunst* (1929), plates B.12, 16, 25, 26; Torr, *op. cit.*, plate 2.

II

The Greek Trireme

The extent of our real knowledge of the Greek trireme is very small. We know that at the time of the Peloponnesian war (431–404 B.C.) each of its oars was worked by one man and can tell by comparing numbers of oars and of crew that this must have been the case for the greater part of the next century. We know that its rowers and their oars were divided into three classes, *thranite*, *zugite* and *thalamite*. We know that in the period 375–330 B.C. the normal complement of oars in an Athenian trireme was 62 thranite, 54 zugite and 54 thalamite, with 30 spares, which might be of two slightly different lengths, roughly 14 and 14½ ft. We know that the oars of the three classes were inventoried separately and that it was possible to confuse those of the thranite and zugite classes. We know that the maximum possible dimensions of an Athenian trireme, as judged from the remains of their slipways, were about 135 ft by 19½ ft.

Anything more has to be inferred from a few references in contemporary literature, from the explanations of the writers of footnotes to that literature or the compilers of dictionaries, all of very much later date, from a very small number of representations of vessels which may or may not be triremes, and finally from considerations of geometry, mechanics and hydrostatics.

Different combinations of knowledge and inference have produced two diametrically opposed schools of thought. In one view all the oars on one side of a trireme were carried in a single horizontal line, but in groups of three; in the other the rowlocks, oar-ports or thole-pins of the thranites formed one line, those of the zugites another and those of the thalamites a third. At one time it was suggested that the essential feature of a trireme was that each of its oars was worked by three men, but this idea is no longer seriously considered.

6

PLATE 1A. Greek bireme, *c.* 550 B.C. British Museum.
From *The Mariner's Mirror*, 1941

PLATE 1B. Phoenician bireme, *c.* 700 B.C. British Museum

PLATE 2A. Lenormant relief, *c.* 400 B.C. Acropolis Museum, Athens

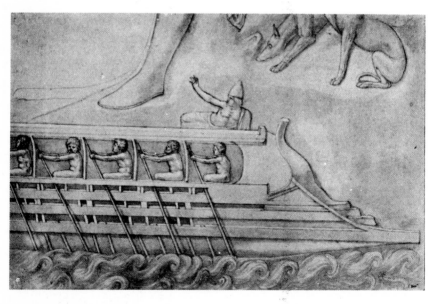

PLATE 2B. Drawing by Cav. dal Pozzo. British Museum

PLATE 3A. Relief from Aquila. National Museum of Aquila

PLATE 3B. Graffito from Delos, copied by Carlini. From *Bulletin de l'Association technique maritime et aéronautique*, 1934

PLATE 4. Palazzo Spada relief. (Vasari)

To my mind the weight of the evidence, such as it is, tells against the first theory. I put it in this way because I must admit that it is far easier to disprove the first than to prove the second. In its purest form the first theory has been most ably set forth by Tarn, with a copious use of literary sources, but with no reference to what others believe to be actual representations of triremes save for a contemptuous denial that they show anything of the sort.[1]

According to Tarn, the Greek trireme of 400 B.C. carried her oars in groups of three all at one level with the thole-pins of each group close together and the three rowers practically side by side. This was the arrangement used by Mediterranean galleys in the first third of the 16th century A.D. and for some 200 years before that. The aftermost oar was slightly the longest and the foremost the shortest; the Venetian names for the three were *piania*, *postizo* and *terzaruol*. One would have expected to find these names equated with the Greek *thranite*, *zugite* and *thalamite*, but this is not what Tarn does. He insists that a Greek trireme's rowers were divided into three squads, forward, amidships and aft, and that all the rowers in the foremost squad were thalamites, those amidships zugites and those aft thranites.

There is a passage in *The Frogs* of Aristophanes which suggests that the thalamites sat close beneath the rowers of one or other of the two remaining classes. Commentators of much later date agree in explaining this by the fact that the thranites sat *ano* and the thalamites *kato*, with the zugites in between. In the natural sense of the two Greek words as given by Liddell and Scott this is a plain statement that the thranites were 'above' and the thalamites 'below'. Tarn, however, takes the two words to mean 'aft' and 'forward' and so justifies his organisation of the rowers in three squads separated by imaginary thwartship lines. He supports this strange interpretation of *ano* and *kato* by a reference in Arrian's *Anabasis* (written in the second century A.D.) to the swamping of some of Alexander's galleys in the rapids of the Hydaspes on account of the nearness of their *kato* oars to the water. One could hardly ask for a more conclusive proof that to Arrian *kato* meant lower, but Tarn takes it as meaning forward and explains that 'the forward oars would of course suffer most in the bad water.'

The galleys in question were *dikrotoi*. The word means literally either double-beating or double-beaten and has usually been taken as equivalent to bireme. If so, and if the *dikrotoi* of Alexander's

[1] *Journal of Hellenic Studies*, 1905, pp. 137, 204; *Hellenistic Military and Naval Developments* (1930); The *Mariner's Mirror*, 1933, p. 52.

flotilla were like the biremes shown in representations of both earlier and later date, there is no difficulty whatever; there were two rows of oars and the water came in beside those of the lower row. Again Tarn avoids the natural interpretation; he accepts *dikrotos* as indicating 'a twofold division of rowers,' but makes that division a matter of forward and aft and uses a very late statement that a *dikrotos* had 'two sets of rowers, as a trireme had three,' to support his own threefold division of a trireme's crew.

The argument, on which he lays great stress, is set out in his *Hellenistic Military and Naval Developments* (p. 162). A papyrus of the first century B.C. shows with fair certainty that a *dikrotos* at that time had a crew of 32 men; she was therefore a *triakonter*, a galley with 30 oars. The relationship between a *dikrotos* and a trireme quoted above from the *Etymologicum Magnum* of about A.D. 1000 involves a division of the former's crew into two sets and the trireme's into three. Since a *triakonter* had only a single row of 15 oars on each side and since no ship has three sides, division into fore (midship) and after squads is the only possibility.

The weak points in this reasoning are obvious. We do not *know* that a *triakonter* was necessarily single-banked; we do not know that all *dikrotoi* were *triakonters*; we certainly cannot be sure that the compiler of the *Etymologicum Magnum* knew anything more about triremes than could be guessed from the word itself, since they had completely disappeared some 600 years before his time.[1] If the story and the explanation prove anything, it is that a *dikrotos* had some oars at a lower level than others and that a trireme went rather farther in that direction. They certainly do not prove Tarn's three-fold fore-and-aft theory.[2]

As I see it, what we know about the numbers and classification of a trireme's oars disposes of this theory once for all. In any arrangement of oars close together in groups of three at one level they must be, as they were in Mediterranean galleys at a much later date, of three different lengths inboard and therefore of different lengths over all, unless the matter of balance and leverage is to be ignored. If so, there must, on Tarn's theory, have been long, medium and short oars in each group; and yet they were distinguished, not by this difference in length, but merely by whether they were used forward, amidships or aft. The suggestion is ridiculous.

A less serious objection can be based on the actual number of oars carried. With 27 thalamite, 27 zugite and 31 thranite oars on

---

[1] Morrison, in *The Mariner's Mirror*, 1941, pp. 15–16.
[2] See also *The Mariner's Mirror*, 1941, p. 319.

each side there would be nine groups of three both forward and amidships and 10 aft, *with a single oar left over*. This cannot be dismissed as actually impossible, but it is certainly most improbable.

Another arrangement with the oars in groups of three very nearly at one level was put forward by A. B. Cook and Wigan Richardson. In this the rowers' seats were slightly staggered, both vertically and horizontally, so that the thranites did indeed sit highest and farthest aft and the thalamites lowest and farthest forward, as required by the commentators' statements already mentioned. It got over the difficulty as to balance and leverage by having a very wide gunwale and staggering the thole-pins in the same way as the seats. As shown in model form this arrangement had the disadvantage of needing more length for the 170 oars than could be provided in a ship able to use the still-existent slipways; otherwise it appears far more reasonable than Tarn's, though it also ignored what may perhaps be called pictorial evidence. In view of the objections which have been urged against the rival theory of superposed banks because of the necessity of putting the thalamite ports at the most 18 in. from the water, it is worth noting that in the Cook-Richardson design the whole freeboard to the gunwale was only 12 in.

This suggested trireme differed from all other designs of the last 70 years or so in having all its thole-pins on the actual gunwale, whereas Tarn puts them all, and the superposed-bank school puts those of the thranite oars, on a sort of continuous straight-sided outrigger projecting some way beyond the gunwale even amidships. Such an outrigger was an invariable feature of Mediterranean galleys for at least the last 500 years of their record and is said to have been first recognised in those of classical times by Assmann in 1887. It will be seen later that Rondolet appears to have made the same discovery as far back as 1820, but this passed unnoticed and it was certainly left for Assmann to identify this outrigger with the Greek word *parekseiresia*, which had previously been taken to mean the space beyond the oars at either end of the ship, not – as is now generally accepted – the space where oars were carried beyond the ship's proper side.

Assmann never followed up his discovery in such a way as to satisfy either school of thought, but he did at least make things easier for those who refused to accept the all-one-level trireme. As long as they had been obliged to put all the oar-ports or thole-pins in the same more or less vertical plane formed by the ship's side, it had proved impossible to devise any arrangement which combined oars of reasonable length and leverage with sufficient room for their rowers to use them. Graser, for instance, had to make his upper rowers sit with their legs wide apart to give room for the heads of those beneath them! With the *parekseiresia* it became possible to place the thranite oars *outside* the zugite and let the two oarsmen sit nearly, if not quite, at the same level and use oars of the same, or almost the same, length and leverage.

Such an arrangement might perhaps have been worked out with no more than the existence of the *parekseiresia* to point the way, but in actual fact there was already evidence which should have put investigators on the right track. In 1852 Lenormant had called attention to a piece of sculpture found on the Acropolis of Athens; this showed a broadside view of a galley of some kind and its probable date, about 400 B.C., suggested a strong probability that the galley was a trireme. Surprisingly little notice was taken of this evidence for a long time. Jal knew of it in 1861, when he wrote *La Flotte de César* and drew Graser's attention to it in time for him to mention it at the end of his *De Veterum Re Navali* in 1864, but it was not generally known until the publication of Cartault's *La Trière Athénienne* in 1881 and even he made little use of it. It was not until 1890 that Kopecky showed that the representation was a sort of scale-drawing and made the first serious attempt at its interpretation.

Kopecky is something of a puzzle. He was, or had been, a captain in the Greek navy; he had carried out experiments in Austrian dockyards and had published some account of his work in a Czech journal; he now wrote in German and dated his preface from Rustchuk in Bulgaria. Marstrand describes him as combining the practical experience of a seaman with 'a comprehensive knowledge of ancient Greek literature.' Bauer, on the other hand, in a review of his book, *Die attischen Trieren,* insisted that he was 'far from having the knowledge required for independent reading and appreciation of ancient writings.'

Whatever his merits as a classical scholar may have been, Kopecky did at least recognise the existence of the outrigger and realise its possibilities. He does not seem to have known of Assmann's recent work and still looked on the *parekseiresia* as the space beyond the oars at either end, but that did not affect his interpretation of the Lenormant relief, though he failed to follow up his own discovery that it was drawn to scale and gave his ship too much freeboard besides making her over-all beam too great. Haack (1895)[1] corrected this and Tenne (1916)[2] was even more careful in the matter of

---

[1] *Uber attische Trieren,* in *Zeitschrift des Vereins deutscher Ingenieure,* Vol. 39.
[2] *Kriegschiffe — — der — — Griechen und Römer.*

scale, but Busley (1920),[1] using Haack's design as the basis of a
model, again exaggerated the freeboard, while Alexanderson (1914)[2]
erred in the opposite direction. Finally, Marstrand (1922)[3] showed
by applying a grid to the relief that all its measurements were very
closely related to that of the *interscalmium*, the distance between two
consecutive thranite thole-pins; the height of the lower side of the
outrigger being, for instance, exactly equal to this, its top 1½ times
and the height of the thalamite ports half of the same basic unit.
This we believe to have been 2 cubits (roughly 38 in. English) and
that value agrees well with the size of the rowers and the probable
length of the longest oars as judged by that of the spares.

Marstrand does not mention Tenne's book, but their two designs
are very much alike, particularly in showing the thranites seated at
the same level as the zugites, whereas most other reconstructions
place them slightly higher. Here, though, attention must be called
to a very remarkable anticipation of these two designs by Rondolet
in 1820,[4] long before the discovery of either the Lenormant relief or
the Athenian dockyard records. One of his suggested thwartship
sections (Fig. 6a) might well be taken for a simplified version of
Tenne's. Unfortunately he gives no more than 'a medal' as his source.

Since Marstrand wrote, Tarn has restated his opinion that the
ship shown in the Lenormant relief is 'a small open galley which
should never have been brought into the business'[5] and has poured
scorn on those who think otherwise; while Carlini has described it
as 'a single-banked vessel', 'a *ponton* intended for some naval festival
or religious ceremony'.[6] On the other hand Morrison has offered a
slight variation on previous interpretations of it as a trireme and
has produced what he believes to be another representation of an
almost exactly similar design.[7] For my part I have ventured to
disagree with both English writers, though chiefly with Tarn.[8]

The new feature about Morrison's trireme is that he makes the
three oars of a group all of one length instead of letting the thalamite
oars be only about two-thirds of the others. His model shows that
this can be done, though only at the cost of putting the blades of
the zugite and thalamite oars dangerously close together in the

[1] *Die Entwicklung des Segelschiffes*, Chapter 4.
[2] *Den Grekiska Trieren*.
[3] *Arsenalet i Piraeus* — —, Chapters 10 and 11.
[4] *Mémoire sur la Marine des Anciens*. I have not seen this book and know of its diagrams only through Marstrand and Kopecky.
[5] *The Mariner's Mirror*, 1933, pp. 65, 458.
[6] *Les Galères antiques*, in *Bulletin de l'Association technique maritime et aéronautique*, 1934.
[7] *The Mariner's Mirror*, 1941, pp. 14–44.
[8] *Ibid.*, pp. 314–323.

water; but whether this arrangement is either necessary or probable is another matter.

Morrison insists that all the oars must be of one length or very nearly so because the only spares recorded differ by only a few inches. This certainly points in that direction, especially in view of the fact that they are called simply 'spares' and not assigned to any particular class. Marstrand suggested that the longer oars would usually break at the thole-pin and that their outboard portions would serve as replacements for those shorter. Perhaps it would be more reasonable to suggest that, provided the spares were long enough, they could be cut down to any length needed, but I must admit that this explanation leaves much to be desired.

On the other hand Morrison does not insist, as others have done, that it is impossible for rowers using oars of different lengths to keep time together. Breusing declared emphatically that this was so and cited the differing periods of short and long pendulums in support of his belief, thus laying himself open to a violent attack by Assman on the ground that an oar is not a free-swinging pendulum but a lever of the first order worked by human strength at one end. Nowadays an oar is more often looked on as a lever of the second order with the blade as its fulcrum, but this makes no difference in the present connection. As long as the relative proportions of their inboard and outboard parts are the same, oars of any length will move a ship or boat the same distance for a given length of travel of the oarsmen's hands and will need the same amount of effort and take the same time over a stroke. The only difference is that shorter oars will travel through a greater angle and will be less efficient because of their tendency to 'pinch the boat' at the beginning of the stroke.

Busley put things very differently; he assumed that all the oars of a trireme travelled through the same angle and showed that in that case the thalamites with their shorter oars would finish their working stroke before either the zugites or the thranites and would have to sit waiting for them to catch up. This is not quite so absurd as the suggestion made by Haweis in an appendix to Vol. 1 of Linday's *History of Merchant Shipping* (1883), that in a quinquereme with five oars in a group two oars made four strokes, two made two and the longest made one, all in the same time; but it is almost as impractical. It would mean either giving the thranites and zugites sliding seats or letting the thalamites take a ridiculously short stroke with their arms only.

There remains the question of the inertia of the oars themselves. If similarly proportioned, two oars whose lengths are as 3 to 2 will differ in weight as 27 to 8, but it is probable that the shorter oars were actually thicker in proportion to their length and had a bigger blade-area. Even so, their weight may well have been only about half that of the others; if the longer oars weighed about 15 lb., the shorter may have weighed some 7 or 8 lb. With both more or less balanced at the thole-pins the difference cannot have been serious. Both Kopecky and Alexanderson claim to have proved the efficiency of their respective designs by experiment, and though it is not quite clear that Kopecky did more than show that the rowers could work without mutual interference, Alexanderson says very definitely that his test was carried out in a boat.

So much for the question whether it is necessary as a matter of mechanics to have all the oars of the same length; now let us see whether it is probable. To my mind we have only to consider the origin of the trireme to dismiss the idea at once. It is almost inconceivable that the very elaborate trireme could have sprung directly from a single-banked galley; it must have been developed from a bireme with oars at two levels by adding the *parekseiresia* to carry the thranite oars and such a bireme would inevitably have had its lower oars shorter than the upper.

Here I must mention the most recent reconstruction of a trireme in Landström's magnificently illustrated book on ships in general.[1] This shows both thranite and zugite oars working through the outrigger close together and at almost the same level with the two rowers seated side by side. One oar is necessarily shorter than the other, while those of the thalamites, working through ports lower down, are shorter still. The design is, in fact, that of the bireme which forms the pedestal of the famous Victory of Samothrace, to be considered in the next chapter, with a third set of oars added lower down to make a trireme. It would clearly work, but I know of no evidence for such a trireme and it cannot be looked on as an interpretation of the Lenormant relief.

At this stage it becomes necessary to consider what the relief actually shows and in doing so it will be convenient to follow Marstrand in converting its measurements into those of a full-size trireme on the assumption that the *interscalmium* represents a length of 2 cubits, 3 ft or 48 in., there having been 16 in. in the Athenian foot. This length corresponds approximately to 38 in. in English measure.

The surviving portion of the relief (Plate 2A) shows nine rowers, the foremost and aftermost much damaged, carved in good proportion to the distance between them and shown in the natural

<hr>

[1] *The Ship*, 1961. Published also in several languages apart from the Swedish original.

attitude for the beginning of a stroke; these are obviously the thranites. They are seated on a level with the upper side of the *parekseiresia* at a height from the waterline of exactly 3 cubits (72 in. Athenian). This *parekseiresia* or outrigger is formed by two longitudinal members with short uprights between them and its depth is 1 cubit. The thranite oars are shown working between the two longitudinals with every third upright acting as a thole-pin. Below the outrigger there are two wales each 8 in. deep with the same distance between them and between the uppermost and the outrigger; this leaves the lower side of the lower wale 1 ft (16 in.) from the waterline. The thalamite oars come from ports just above this lower wale and almost directly beneath the thranite tholes, while the zugite oars appear from beneath the outrigger and are shown slightly nearer to the thranite oars than to the thalamite.

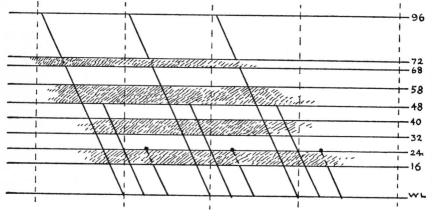

FIG. 2. *Trireme as shown in the Lenormant relief*

Besides the oars there are other lines more or less parallel with them running from the top of the lower wale to the outrigger and starting from the wale a little abaft the thalamite ports. These and a series of less well defined lumps just before them between the upper wale and the outrigger have been taken to represent struts and brackets. There is also a covering over the rowers' heads supported by stanchions which appear to curve aft at the top. It seems likely that the curve was really outwards and that its shape and the slanting of the lower struts is due to an attempt to introduce perspective by shifting the viewpoint slightly before the beam.

Fig. 2 shows the apparent disposition of the oars in a purely diagrammatic way, though the proportions are those of the relief itself; while Fig. 3 is an attempt to draw a possible midship section.

All attempts since Kopecky's have inevitably been somewhat similar, but it is possible to divide them into four groups. Tenne and Marstrand seat the thranites and zugites at the same level, whereas all other designs put the thranites a little higher. Haack and Alexanderson put the thalamites exactly under the thranites, Busley's modification of Haack's design puts them slightly farther inboard and Morrison, wishing to make all oars the same length, has to seat them in the same fore-and-aft plane as the zugites.

My own version comes very near to Busley's, but has the outrigger a good deal wider, so that the thranites sit farther from the zugites in a thwartship sense. This makes it possible to carry the inner ends of separate thranite seats on a fore-and-after running above the zugite oars instead of making the thranite rowers sit

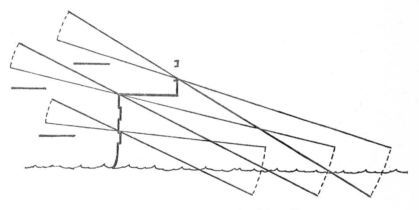

FIG. 3. *Section of trireme deduced from Fig. 2*

astride a single long plank. In theory this seems to be an improvement, but it would be foolish to dogmatise without having built and tested a full-size reconstruction of at least two complete groups of oars.

The Lenormant relief has a pair of rather dubious relatives. Among the 17th-century drawings of Greek and Roman antiquities by Cavaliere dal Pozzo, now in the British Museum, there is one (Plate 2B) which appears at first sight to show the bow of the same galley; while a fragment in the Museum at Aquila in Italy (Plate 3A) might be taken as showing its last four rowers towards the stern. Unfortunately closer examination shows that these two representations differ in several places both from the Lenormant relief and from one another. Figs. 4 and 5 are drawn in the same way as

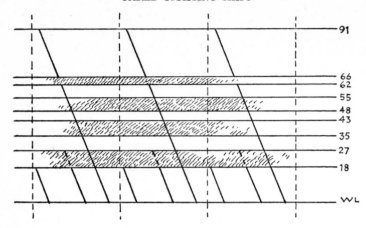

FIG. 4. *Trireme as shown in the Pozzo drawing*

Fig. 2 with the *interscalmium* and the height of the lower side of the *parekseiresia* taken to be the same in each case. It will be seen at once that the other proportions differ and that the treatment of the zugite and thalamite oars differs still more. Pozzo shows both appearing from *below* the lower wale, though the thalamite oars point to lumps above that wale exactly as they do in the relief and can fairly be claimed to have had their ports there in the same way. Aquila, on the other hand, takes both right up to the outrigger. The explanation must be that the two sculptors concerned – or perhaps in one case the later draughtsman – copied something very

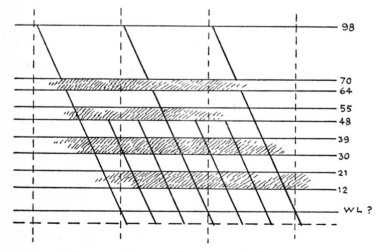

FIG. 5. *Trireme as shown in the Aquila sculpture*

like the Lenormant relief and made the two possible mistakes, one transforming the upper part of the zugite oars into a second set of struts, the other taking the normal struts as prolongations of the thalamite oars.

The ship on the Talos vase,[1] believed by Morrison to be a trireme of almost the same design as that in the Lenormant relief, can certainly be interpreted in that way with the aid of a good deal of adjustment and imagination, but if the relief had not been at hand, it is very doubtful whether anyone would have recognised the possibilities of the vase; for the ship, and indeed the whole composition, is remarkably like that on the 'Ficoronische Ciste' reproduced by Köster[2] and that could never be taken for a trireme at first sight.

The same may be said of the terracotta trireme found in Egypt in 1903 and now in the Danish National Museum. Alexanderson reproduced a photograph of this much battered object, but described it as roughly and carelessly made with no claim to be considered a trustworthy representation of its subject. My own verdict would be even more harsh; it *may* be meant for a trireme, but there is nothing whatever to be learnt from it.

There remains the indisputable 3-level galley included among the *graffiti* on the island of Delos, but here we find an unfortunate difference of opinion as regards its date. Carlini, who published a tracing from this design (Plate 3B), considered that it could hardly have been executed much before the middle of the first century B.C.,[3] and though Köster, presumably writing about the same series of drawings, puts them back to the middle of the 3rd century,[4] they would even then have been made at a time when triremes, though still in use, had been outclassed by heavier galleys. Still, one thing is certain, we can take it as proved that a reconstruction of a trireme with three distinct rows of oars, as deduced from the Lenormant relief, is not the impossiblity that the believers in the all-one-level theory have declared it to be.[5]

At the beginning of this chapter the maximum possible dimensions of an Athenian trireme were given as about 135 ft by 19½ ft English. It now becomes necessary to see whether the 'accepted' interpretation of the Lenormant relief can produce a vessel of suitable size. The difference between the width over all and the true beam suggested in Fig. 3 is 5¼ ft; this points to a beam for the actual hull of about

---

[1] *The Mariner's Mirror*, 1941, Plate 3.
[2] *Das antike Seewesen* (1923), p. 115.
[3] *Op. cit.*, pp. 60 and 78.
[4] *Op. cit.*, p. 114 note.
[5] This galley will be mentioned again in the next chapter.

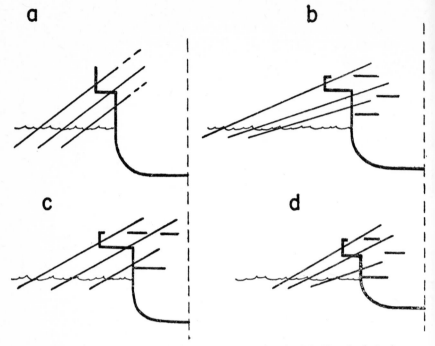

FIG. 6. *Sections of triremes as given by* (a) *Rondolet* (*1820*), (b) *Kopecky* (*1890*), (c) *Tenne* (*1916*), (d) *Haack* (*1896*)

14 ft, which is much the same as that proposed by other modern students. For the length we have to take 30 times the *interscalmium* of 38 in. – 95 ft – and make an allowance for the ends beyond the rowers. This can hardly be less than about 35 ft, say, 20 ft forward and 15 ft aft, if the lines are to be kept reasonably sharp, and gives a total length of 130 ft. The result is therefore a vessel just small enough to be accommodated on the slipway and just large enough to find room for her 170 rowers.

We have no direct knowledge of the appearance of a trireme as a whole, since even the Delos drawing shows only the aftermost two thirds of the ship, but we can be fairly sure of it because of the close similarity of representations of galleys of both earlier and later date. Fig. 7 shows – purely diagrammatically – a trireme in broadside view.[1]

As to its construction we know even less, but we have reason to believe that the hull was carvel-built with planks fitted edge to edge and an inner structure of keel, ribs and beams. The earlier

[1] For a more artistic drawing see the Science Museum's *Sailing Ships*, Vol. 1, Plate 4.

Egyptian style of building, in which thick planking was dowelled together with a minimum of internal timbering, would have been too heavy and at the same time too weak for a long narrow vessel meant for use in open water and called on to withstand the shock of using the ram.

This use of the ship as a weapon in itself was the factor on which the whole design of a trireme was based. The ram had been a feature of fighting ships for at least two or three centuries before the appearance of the trireme in about 500 B.C. and there are suggestions of it in the few small representations which we have of Cretan ships of much earlier date, but it was in the days of the trireme that its importance was greatest. After that, with ships growing heavier and heavier, naval warfare became more a matter of land-fighting at sea and the ram, though still retained, became something of a survival.

Its presence entailed the complete differentiation of bow and stern. Egyptian ships had been almost uniformly double-ended for

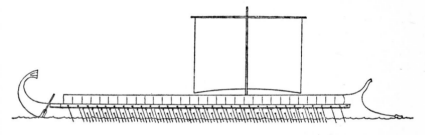

FIG. 7. *Conjectural broadside view of trireme*

a thousand years or more, and though sculptures of soon after 1200 B.C. do show the bow cut off short and fitted with some kind of beast's head, this is too far from the water to be looked on as a true ram and has not caused any real change from the normal spoon-like shape of both ends of the ship. Greek fighting ships from about 700 B.C. – and perhaps their Cretan ancestors – show something very different; the keel runs up in a gentle curve to the waterline to meet the converging lower wales in a point finished off, at least in later examples, by a more or less faithful representation of an animal's snout, presumably in metal.

Above the ram the profile of the stem was concave and passed gradually to the vertical, ending in an upward projection of no apparent use, sometimes a mere post, but more often suggestive of the trunk of a trumpeting elephant. Abaft this there was something in the nature of a forecastle reaching as far as the beginning of the space occupied by the rowers, at which point there were two heavy projecting timbers, usually considered as catheads, but more probably serving to protect the end of the outrigger or to damage that of an opponent. The only other feature of note was another projection sometimes shown above the actual ram. This, the *proembolon*, whereas the ram was called the *embolon*, was probably a kind of buffer intended to prevent the penetration of an enemy's hull from being deep enough to endanger the ramming vessel.

At the other end of the ship the stern was not unlike an exaggerated version of the bow or stern of a Canadian canoe, the sternpost with its decorative finish rising high above the rest of the hull and curving through an arc not far short of a semicircle. Here, at the after end of the *parekseiresia*, were the two great steering-oars, or rather side-rudders, which were still to be found in Mediterranean craft for another 1,800 years or so.

The Lenormant relief and its relatives show a light deck above the rowers of the topmost bank, but nothing to shield them from the side, and the Delos drawing suggests much the same thing. We know, however, that some sort of light protection was soon added here and that this improvement was retained in the many-banked galleys of the Hellenistic age. Ships with such protection for their rowers were said to be *kataphract*.

The trireme's remoter ancestors must have been purely rowing vessels, but there is no doubt that all sea-going craft had carried sail for centuries, though there had been no question of fighting save under oars. The sail, which in so narrow and unstable a ship could only be used with a fair wind, was a rather shallow square sail set on a mast about two-fifths of the ship's length from the bow. The mast could be lowered and both mast and sail were left ashore, if possible, before going into battle, but a smaller sail set on a mast raking over the stem almost like a very heavily steeved bowsprit was retained for use in emergencies such as an attempted escape from pursuit with the oars more or less disabled.

III

Quinqueremes and Polyremes

The standard fighting ship of the Peloponnesian war (431–404 B.C.) had been the trireme; in the first Punic war (264–241) it was the quinquereme, whose oar-power must, from the two names, have been related to that of the trireme in some way as 5 is to 3. At first sight this suggests quite a slow process of development, but actually Carthage and Rome seem to have failed to keep up with the times and to have been using ships much smaller than some of those built in the eastern basin of the Mediterranean in the third century B.C. and the first half of the second.

Quadriremes, or in the Greek form *tetrereis* (4's) are said to have been introduced at Syracuse in 398 B.C. and 5's soon after, with 6's appearing about 350. Doubt has been cast on these dates, but it is known that there were 5's in Phoenicia and in Cyprus by 332 and that Athens had 4's before 330 and 5's in 325. Then came Demetrios Poliorcetes of Macedon and with him the era of bigger and bigger ships; he had 7's before 306, an 11 and a 13 within the next five years and a 15 and a 16 by 288. At the same time Lysimachos of Thrace had a big ship built at Heraklea on the Black Sea. This is called an 8, but it has been argued that it was really a 16; while the same has been suggested with regard to the *Isthmia*, in which Antigonos Gonatas, son of Demetrios, fought and won the battle of Kos in 256. Such information as we have points to her having been a 9 on some new plan, but here again at least one writer has wished to double that number. Meanwhile in Egypt the first two Ptolemys had built 7's, 9's, 11's and 13's, followed before 246 by a 20 and a 30. The culmination of the series was the 40 built by Ptolemy III. about 215, and though this was certainly not a practical sea-going ship, it has its importance, because we know something of its dimensions.

It must be evident that the numerals cannot possibly be taken as indicating the number of separate horizontal rows of oars. A trireme did have its three longitudinal banks, or so most people now believe; but to think of anything of the sort in a class higher than, perhaps, a quinquereme is out of the question. Attempts to design 'polyremes'[1] on these lines have been merely ludicrous.

The only satisfactory explanation is that the numerals indicate the number of men employed on each group of oars, the 'half room' of Viking ships. This has at least the virtue of being both inclusive and non-commital; it can be accepted equally well by those who still cling to the doctrine of 'one man, one oar,' by those who believe that a 7, for example, had that number of men on each large oar, and by those who think that a group might contain two or more oars of different lengths with crews of different numbers of men.

Of these rival theories the first may safely be ignored and the second has to be merged in the third long before the progression reaches its climax, because it would be impossible to employ more than a certain number of men effectively on a single oar. The limit was probably about 10 and whatever the system used in the larger 'polyremes' may have been, it must have involved the combination of at least two oars and possibly three in each group.

One of our few scraps of real knowledge is that the oars of an Athenian trireme could be transferred to a 4 and those of a 4 to a 5, but unfortunately this information belongs to the very beginning of the period under consideration and give us little help in deciding how nearly the Roman quinquereme of 250 B.C. resembled the Athenian pentere of 75 years earlier. On the whole it seems probable that they differed far less than the holders of the big-oar theory would have us believe.

In any case, we are bound to start by considering what these early 4's and 5's were like. Was a 4 simply a 3 with a slight increase in beam and an extra man on each oar of one bank and was a 5 formed from a 4 in the same way, or was it a matter of adding a fourth and a fifth oar to each group of three? The first alternative appears simple at first sight, but would involve discarding some third of a trireme's oars in the shift to a 4 and a similar loss in the transfer from a 4 to a 5. It has been suggested that the oars were actually lengthened on their inboard portions, but it is hard to believe that this was a practical possibility.

If an entire set of oars could be promoted to a higher class, we have to turn to the second alternative and consider how room could be found for another one-man oar in each group. Here it must be admitted that those who believe that a trireme's three oars were

[1] This is a hybrid word like 'television', but I prefer it to 'multiremes.'

placed side by side at one level have an advantage over their opponents, since all that would be necessary would be to fit a fourth thole-pin close abaft the third and provide another oar about 1½ ft longer inboard, as was actually done in Venice in the early part of the 16th century. There are, however, far too many objections to the all-one-level theory to let us take this easy course; these have been set out at length in the chapter dealing with triremes.

On the other hand, how a fourth bank of oars could be added to groups arranged as in the usual interpretation of the Lenormant relief is a very difficult problem. Attempts have been made to solve it by seating another set of rowers directly above the zugites and putting their thole-pins in the spaces between those of the thranites and well above them; while another possibility would be to widen the outrigger and seat the new rowers farther from the middle-line than the thranites. Such suggestions are, however, no more than geometrical exercises; there is no evidence that they even approach the truth.

It may be that these speculations have been unnecessary and that the first alternative should not have been dismissed so lightly. A trireme's full complement of oars, excluding spares, was 170, but as a rule nearly half that number were written off each year, leaving no more than would equip two banks, if that, and allowing the third to receive new oars of the greater length needed for a two-man crew. This explanation is no more than a guess, but it can at least be claimed that there is nothing to prove the guess wrong and that is more than can be said for some rival theories. If early Athenian 4's and 5's were indeed derived directly from triremes, they must, I think, have been produced in this way.

How far evolution could go on these lines is hard even to guess. A pentere with two men on each of the two uppermost oars of a group would still be fairly close to the parent stock and one can imagine something similar with 3–2–1 or 2–2–2 men to an oar, this last being simply a double-banked trireme, using the term in the modern sense of having two men on each oar in place of one; but it is a long way from there to the 15 and even that is by no means the end of the series. My own view, and here for once I agree with Tarn, is that the 6's and 7's used by Demetrios in 306 B.C. introduced a drastic change of design and that it was from them that the later great ships were developed.

It is easy to say that there must have been a drastic change, but it is far from easy, for me at least, to say what that change was. Tarn has no difficulty; it was a matter of abandoning the system of one-man oars – all at one level – and substituting a single row of larger oars each worked by several men, the same change as was made in Venice in the first half of the 16th century A.D. In his own words: 'With the quinquereme we are on firm ground . . . She was rowed by a single row of oars through an outrigger with five men to each oar.' He also says: 'It is certain that from quinqueremes up to 10's the numbers mean so many men to an oar; a 7 had a single row of oars with seven men at each, a 10 had a single row with 10 men at each.'[1]

His chief evidence for the single row of oars was that Livy, when describing the removal of the oars on one side of a quinquereme, to let two of them be lashed side by side, wrote *ordo remorum* (row of oars) not *ordines* in the plural, 'as he must have done if there had been several rows or banks of oars.' I once suggested that *ordo remorum* might mean simply 'set of oars,' but this Tarn would not accept. Unfortunately I then missed another passage quoted by Tarn himself,[2] in which Livy mentions the fact that a Roman quinquereme was worked *pluribus remorum ordinibus* (by more rows of oars) than a Carthaginian trireme. That must entail at least two rows, even if the trireme in question did carry her oars all at one level, which is most unlikely.

Tarn also laid stress on a passage in which Appian describes the inexperienced rowers of certain galleys as being unable to stand steady at their work in rough water. He made two assumptions which can be accepted without demur, 'that for serious work no man ever stood at an oar if he could possibly sit and that five men to one oar cannot all sit through the stroke.' Therefore, he said, these vessels must have had a single row of oars worked by several men each. That may be so, but two things must be remembered; Appian is dealing with events of as late as 42 B.C. and he gives no clue to the class of the galleys in question save that they were larger than their opponents. He cannot be taken as proving anything whatever as regards the quinqueremes of the two Punic wars.

What these were really like is uncertain and in the absence of new evidence must remain so. One cannot dismiss the single row of five-man oars as impossible, for it was the normal practice in the galleys of the 17th century A.D.; but still less can one accept it as the inevitable or even the most likely arrangement. In my view, the Roman or Carthaginian quinquereme was probably worked by two rows of oars, the longer handled by three men and the shorter by two. Whether these two rows were at noticeably different levels with their ports staggered as in the early biremes, or whether Tenne

[1] *The Mariner's Mirror*, 1933, pp. 67 and 70.
[2] *Journal of Hellenic Studies*, 1905, p. 156.

was right in proposing something very like a Greek trireme with the thalamite oars removed,[1] I do not know. On the whole I prefer the second alternative, though I should find it hard to give my reasons for doing so.

Leaving the western Mediterranean and its quinqueremes we come to the 'great ships' or 'polyremes' of the Hellenistic navies. Three well known pieces of sculpture are generally recognised as showing galleys of this period, but it is far from certain that they represent the great ships whose nature is so difficult to understand. The most important, because it is three-dimensional, not merely a relief, is the pediment of the Victory of Samothrace, now in the Louvre (*Frontispiece*), and this has been the subject of nearly as much disagreement as the Lenormant trireme. That the sculpture shows the goddess Nike on the forecastle of a galley and that it commemorates some important battle is universally accepted, but what battle is uncertain and what kind of galley still more so.

At one time the victory was believed to be that of Demetrios Poliorcetes at Salamis (Cyprus) in 306 B.C.; now his son Antigonos Gonatas and the battle of Kos in 258 are considered more likely. If the monument shows the victorious flagship, as has been claimed, the matter of date is important, because Demetrios fought in a 7 and Antigonos in the new-fashioned 9 (or possibly 18) already mentioned. Writing in 1905 Tarn asked: 'How can the prow of Samothrace represent anything but Demetrius' hepteres any more than a moment of Trafalgar could represent any ship but the *Victory*?'[2] and yet in 1933 he described the monument as probably the prow of Gonatas's 18 'simplified for artistic reasons.'[3] It is true that by then he had abandoned his earlier belief that this 18 (or 9) and the 16 (or 8) of Lysimachos 'were abnormal in some way in their oarage,' but even so the sudden switch from a 7 to an 18 demanded more in the way of justification.

The more usual view is that the vessel represented is quite a small galley, 'the light swift despatch-boat from the victorious fleet' and that the monument may even be an actual full-size reproduction in stone of part of such a boat. The fact that Demetrios is known to have sent his biggest ship home with the good news tells against this interpretation, but by no means decisively; the artist may well have thought a small ship better suited to his composition or may even have been giving his version of 'Nike's own ship,' as Torr suggested.

---

[1] *Kriegschiffe — — der — — Griechen und Römer* (1916), Plate 6.
[2] *Journal of Hellenic Studies*, 1905, p. 208.
[3] *The Mariner's Mirror*, 1933, p. 70; *Hellenistic Military and Naval Developments*, p. 137 note.

One extraordinary piece of criticism must be mentioned. Breusing denied that the thing was meant for a ship or boat of any kind and quoted 'experienced seamen' as calling it 'a piano, a writing desk, a skate or a sausage-machine', but never thinking of a ship!

This astonishing outburst need not be taken seriously, but the interpretation as a small bireme, probably reproduced full-size, demands careful study. From Carlini's scale-drawings we find that the greatest width at the level of the thole-pins is approximately 7 ft 10½ in. He adheres to this in his suggested section, and though he insists that the galley has been reproduced in its actual size, he has to admit that it would be necessary to add 10 per cent everywhere 'to let the rowers be comfortable'.[1] Assmann went a little further as regards the width and made it almost 9 ft,[2] but it may be that he thought it might have been that much greater amidships. Voigt copied Assmann's section and its scale without comment and thought also that the sculpture was full-size, but went on to give a suggested reconstruction of the whole ship with a beam of almost 20 ft and that apparently for the main hull only without the out-riggers! At the same time he offered a plan view including four rowers and went out of his way to exchange the positions of the two banks, putting the shorter oar abaft the longer and thus making the inner man's oar pass between the hands and the body of his neighbour!

Carlini's section appears just possible, though his two rowers would have to sit remarkably close together and even so the outer man would be too close to his thole to do much useful work. It has, however, the great merit of putting the ship deep enough in the water to make it look likely to float the right way up and to bring the probable position of the ram down to the waterline. Assmann's ship is shown floating 1½ ft lighter; it looks thoroughly unstable and would, as Voigt's sheer-plan shows, have had its ram well in the air.

If we abandon the despatch-boat idea for the moment and accept Tarn's two claims, that the ship represented is the flagship of Antigonos Gonatas and that this vessel ended her days in the great dock-house on Delos, which could accommodate a ship nearly 29 ft wide, we have to take the scale as about ⅓ and at once find ourselves confronted by oar-ports about 3 ft long and 1 ft deep. As they appear on the monument they would be large enough to take any oar of reasonable size, even one from a galeass of the 17th century;

---

[1] *Les Galères antiques.* In *Bulletin de l'Assosiation technique maritime et aéronautique*, 1934, pp. 73-4, Plates E and F.

[2] *Seewesen*, in Baumeister's *Denkmäler*, p. 1633.

[3] *Der Schiffsbug von Samothrake* — —. In *Schiffsbau*, 1912, p. 559.

multiplied by three they become ridiculous. This drives us back to the idea of a smaller vessel reproduced full-size, though it is hard to accept that unreservedly. Just possible as a matter of three-dimensional space, provided the inhabitants of the Levant in those days were small enough, it is still sufficiently awkward to suggest that the sculptor must have made his ship too narrow 'for artistic reasons.' Certainly an increase in beam without a corresponding increase in depth would produce a far more stable craft.

Whatever her class, this stone-ship shows one feature which cannot be ignored; it shows a pair of oar-ports close together and staggered so that the aftermost overlaps the foremost at a very slightly higher level. This points unmistakably to a pair of oars, whether worked by one man each or by several, close enough together to make it necessary to give the aftermost greater length inboard than the other and seat (or stand) its crew nearer the midship line. The arrangement must, in fact, have been that of the Cook-Richardson trireme with one of its three banks omitted.

This, as I understand it, is how Tarn believed the oars were disposed in galleys of classes from 11 to 20 inclusive. Would it be possible on such a system as this to keep the beam of the 18 down to, say, 28 ft to let her fit into the Delos dock? Could 18 men be usefully employed on two closely spaced oars of which the longer was only about 13 ft long inboard? It must be remembered that, although it would be possible to put some of the crew of the longer oar on its after side and let them push instead of pulling, this could not be done on the shorter forward oar. However the two crews were divided there must have been at least 10 men to be fitted in side by side on the fore side of the pair. To put any of them nearer to the thole-pin than 3 ft or more would be out of the question and that leaves 10 ft at most for the same number of men, a completely inadequate amount. It has been suggested as an alternative that the dock may have housed the 15 taken from Demetrios and dedicated by Ptolemy some 70 years before the battle of Kos, but that is hardly more possible. On any system of pairs of oars at, or nearly at, the same level, the Delos dock might perhaps have taken an 11, but nothing larger.

That some galleys did have their oars so arranged cannot be denied. The 'Victory prow' is amply corroborated by what is known as the Palazzo Spada relief, in which we see the stern of a galley and the aftermost 14 oars, grouped in pairs with the aftermost oar of each pair appearing through the *parekseiresia* very slightly higher than the other (Plate 4). A second version of the same subject from the Villa Ludovisi cannot now be traced, but has been well reproduced.[1] In it the pairing and staggering of the oars has been omitted, but otherwise the resemblance is very close indeed. Tarn described these two reliefs in 1905 as 'Roman copies of some Hellenistic original' and then considered that 'the ship may have been a bireme, but may just as well have had several men to an oar.' He does not seem to have noticed the difference between the two versions in the treatment of the oars. By 1933 he had excluded the bireme and described the ship as 'some great cataphract which was something bigger than a 10,' because he then believed that anything up to a 10 had only a single row of oars and that a vessel with the rowers hidden (a cataphract) must be at least a trireme.

His authority for this last statement was very slight; but, even if it were true, it hardly seems applicable. The sculptor might well have shown the rowers, if his skill had been equal to it, since the structure above the double line of oars is no more than an open-work grid, certainly not solid enough to let us be sure that he was representing a 'great cataphract.' On the whole it seems more likely that the galley is a small one. It would be foolish to press the matter of scale too far, but the relative size of such things as the pilot's shelter, the spears or standards and – in the Ludovisi version – the tiller, strongly suggests that the actual ship was not very large.

Returning to the *Isthmia* of Antigonos Gonatas. All that we know of her design is contained in an untranslatable sentence which still makes it clear that she had 'some ninefold arrangement of oars and more than one *katastroma* (upper deck).' Similarly the great ship of Lysimachos is described as an 8 with two *katastromata*, though the enemies she was intended to meet included at least one 13. It has been suggested, as mentioned already, that this ship was really a 16 and the *Isthmia* an 18, but there is no justification for this; the former is called quite definitely 'the lion-bearing 8'.

Now the *Isthmia* is also described by the single word *triarmenos*. This means literally 'three-fitted' and is used elsewhere in the sense both of three-masted and of three-decked. Here, the only time we find it used of a galley, there is more than a temptation to take it as meaning three-banked and to look on the ship as a kind of over-grown trireme with three oars in a group and nine men employed on them in place of three.

Is it possible that the apparent trireme of Delos mentioned in the previous chapter is such a vessel as this; not necessarily the *Isthmia* herself, but a three-level polyreme of some kind? The idea may seem far-fetched, but it would at least help to get over the

---

[1] See Moll, *Das Schiff in der bildenden Kunst* (1929), Plate B.IV.113 (photograph) or Köster, *op. cit.*, p. 141 (line).

difficulty of explaining why the artist should have drawn a type of galley which had long been outclassed.

The two descriptions, such as they are, suggest that the 8 from Heraklea was similar to the *Isthmia* in design and that they both differed from the general run of galleys up to then. This brings up the question whether such a new-type 8 could be a sufficient answer to the 13 which Lysimachos had seen in the navy of Demetrios. So far each step forward from the original single-banked galley had been a matter of getting more power by increasing the number of rowers in a given length of hull. At first sight the change from groups of 13 men to eight looks like a step in the wrong direction, but there are other factors to be taken into account apart from the mere numerical relationship. The big oars of a 13 were probably manned on both sides and that would involve increasing the space between groups by some 50 per cent. This means that 26 men on the one system – two groups – would occupy as much length as 24 in a new-style 8 or 27 in a 9. At the same time allowance must be made for the fact that pushing is less effective than pulling; the efficiency of a man pushing on an oar has been estimated at ¾ of that of one pulling, but is probably less. If only four men out of the 13 pushed, the power would come down at least to 12, while the lighter oars of an 8, manned perhaps by 3–3–2 men each, all pulling, would of themselves be more efficient. Add to this the consideration that an 8 need not be as wide as a 13 and it will be seen that she might be both faster and handier than a larger galley of the old type.

This matter of width is important. We have seen that the *Isthmia*, as a normal 18, could not have been placed in the dock-house on Delos, but we can now see that, as a trireme fashion 9, this would have been possible. Take 18 ft for the space occupied by 12 men, the thranites and zugites, add twice 4 ft for the distance of the outermost rowers from their thole-pins and 2 ft for a central fore-and-aft gangway, and the result is just the 28 ft needed. If the Delos dock did indeed house the *Isthmia*, she must have been designed in some such way as this.

Setting aside these two ships as possibly abnormal in the arrangement of their oars we still have to consider their predecessors, contemporaries and successors, galleys ranging upwards from 5's to 15, 16, 20, 30 and 40. In view of the fact that the 8 followed the 13 and the 9 came long after the 15 and 16, but before the 20, there is a temptation to think that there was indeed a steady numerical progression and that, whereas the 8 and 8 were classed by the number of rowers on one side, the 'half room,' the other included those on both sides. This would make the 16 into an 8, the 20 into a 10 and so on and would certainly make the larger classes easier to accept.

When I first put forward this suggestion,[1] I was under the impression that Lysimachos's 8 was actually called a 16 in some accounts and that the same thing occurred in the case of the *Isthmia*. Here I seem to have been misled; the alternative classification of the 'lion-bearing 8' as a 16 depends solely on the remote possibility that she may have been the same vessel as the 16 which Demetrios is known to have possessed in 288 B.C. and even the same as the 16 which was in the navy of Philip V in 197 and was taken to Rome in 168; while that of the *Isthmia* is no more than a claim by Tarn that she must have been an 18 because she was an advance on the 16.

There is, in any case, a decisive argument against the idea of counting both sides in the fact that so many of the classes recorded are named by *odd* numbers. It might perhaps be thought that a change of classification came in after the appearance of the highest numbered of these, the 15, but this is easily disproved by a consideration of Ptolemy V's celebrated 40. If she had 4,000 rowers, as we are told, there must have been 2,000 on either side and thus 50 groups of 40; this is reasonably compatible with her reputed length of 420 ft, but 100 groups of 20 is out of the question. In her case at least the old system of classification must have been used, and if a 40 was actually built, we can hardly deny the possibility of a 30 or a 20 however difficult it may be to understand them.

Real evidence as to the arrangement of the oars in these last of the great galleys is almost as scanty as that bearing on the quinquereme and it is far harder to base any argument on what appears to be possible. Tarn pointed out that their classification depends on multiples of 10 and by combining this fact with the belief – probably well founded – that 10 men were as many as could usefully be stationed at a single oar made the 20 have two oars in a group, the 30 three and the 40 four. In this I would be prepared to follow him, if necessary, though I cannot believe, as he does, that these groups of oars had their thole-pins close together. That seems to me quite impossible.

[1] *The Mariner's Mirror*, 1941, p. 313.

IV

Liburnians and Dromons

When we consider how much we know of Roman history, it seems very strange that we should know so little about Roman fighting ships. Of sailing merchantmen we have a fair knowledge, but of rowing men-of-war we know far less. What the quinqueremes of the first Punic war were like is still a matter of dispute and there is the same uncertainty about the ships which fought at Actium in 31 B.C. and their successors during the next few centuries.

The battle of Actium was one of the few occasions on which comparatively small ships defeated larger opponents. The losing fleet consisted mainly of galleys ranging from 4's to 10's, while the winners had nothing larger than 6's and were chiefly triremes and liburnians, which seem to have been smaller still.

The only thing certain about the liburnian is that it first came to the front as the type of vessel used by the pirates of the Dalmatian coast and that it was faster and handier than the normal fighting galley. Torr puts its adoption in the Roman navy about 50 B.C. and describes it as 'two-banked,' but offers no suggestion as to how these banks were arranged. Tenne has no doubt whatever; in his view it was simply a matter of omitting the thalamite oars of a trireme and retaining those of the two upper banks.[1] The suggestion is reasonable enough, but he spoils his case by claiming that the quinqueremes built by the Romans towards the end of the first Punic war were of 'liburnian design.' It is quite likely that these quinqueremes did have oars corresponding to the thranite and zugite oars of a trireme, with three men on one and two on the other, but they were not liburnians. As to these there is no way of knowing whether they were Greek triremes without the thalamite oars or something more like the galley shown on the Victory pediment. My own preference is for the second alternative, but only

[1] *Kriegschiffe — — der Griechen und Römer*, p. 69 and Plate 6.

because certain rather unsatisfactory representations of galleys which *may* be liburnians are more easily explained as being built in that way.

A piece of sculpture found on the site of the temple of Fortuna at Praeneste and now in the Vatican is generally accepted as showing a galley of suitable date to have fought at Actium (Plate 5A). It has been considered and reproduced by many writers and they have reached almost as many different conclusions as to the size and class of the ship represented and the arrangement of its oars. Torr calls it simply a 'Roman bireme' and in the sense that it has two distinct rows of oars this is true. Casson, the most recent writer on the subject, makes it 'one of the heavy ships that fought at Actium' and notes that 'the vessel has two banks of oars, each oar manned by multiple rowers.'[1] Rodgers, on the other hand, believes it to be one of Agrippa's ships 'of a rather small type' with a lower bank of oars each worked by one man and an upper bank with two men on each.[2] Tenne starts by claiming that the vessel is obviously Cleopatra's flagship and suggesting that the artist must have seen it drawn up on the beach at Alexandria. He goes on to insist that what looks like mere decoration above the oars is really a series of blades of oars pulled inboard, and that when the artist decided to show the oars of the two lowest banks in their working position, he forgot to remove two out of every three of these blade-ends.[3] Köster followed him to some extent, but described the ship as having one thalamite, one zugite and two thranite banks, 'because the upper oars, of which only the ends appear, are shown in double number.'[4] I must admit having at one time accepted this idea of oar-blades looking like decoration, but I now feel almost sure that I was wrong. There are neither three nor two blades shown for each oar in the bank below, but roughly five for every three. This might perhaps be explained by putting pairs of thranite oars 4 ft apart and single oars beneath them at the normal spacing of about 3 ft 4 in., but there is no suggestion whatever of pairing in the way these upper blades are shown.

With such differences of opinion as to what the sculpture really shows it is not surprising that there should be similar disagreement in estimates of size and of number of rowers in a group. Rodgers makes the ship a two-banked 3, Köster a 4 with one man on each oar; Tenne gives each of three oars two men and so produces a 6; Casson does not commit himself, but his use of the word 'multiple'

[1] *The Ancient Mariners* (1959), Plate 10.
[2] *Greek and Roman Naval Warfare* (1937), pp. 514-6.
[3] *Op cit.*, pp. 52-5 and Plate 7.
[4] *Das antike Seewesen* (1923), p. 150.

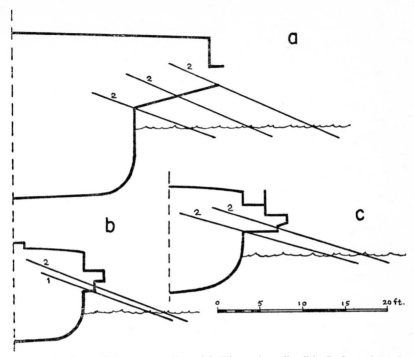

Fig. 8. *Sections of Praeneste galley:* (a) *Tenne* (*1916*), (b) *Rodgers* (*1937*), (c) *Anderson* (*1962*)

suggests an 8 or even a 10. As to size the variation is best illustrated by a comparison of Tenne's and Rodgers's midship sections drawn on the same scale (Fig. 8). To these I have added my own interpretation of the ship as a two-banked 4, but I would not claim that this is more than a reasonable possibility.

Another carving found more recently near Ostia (Plate 5B) is quite as hard to explain. One thing at least is certain; it shows oars working through ports at three levels. Even Tarn, who denied that oars could be worked through ports and declared that 'there is no monument of any kind or any period which shows superimposed banks',[1] would have had to reconsider his position in face of this new evidence.

At first sight it looks as if the oars are in the side of the true hull with an apparently purposeless outrigger above them, but closer examination shows that there is in fact an outrigger in two steps, as in the Praeneste ship, and that the oars emerge from its lower, less prominent part.

[1] *The Mariner's Mirror*, 1933, p. 52.

The sculpture is probably quite unreliable in its proportions, but it is evident that the vertical distance between ports must have been very small. As far as I can see, we have to accept something like the arrangement shown on the Victory pediment or on one of the two 'Roman copies of a Hellenistic original' (Tarn) mentioned in the previous chapter, but with three oars in a group instead of two. Admittedly the carving shows the ports almost exactly one above another, but the oars themselves appear in a way which would be impossible if that were the case. As a matter of fact such a grouping of three oars is not beyond possibility. Galleys of much later date were rowed by oars grouped in threes horizontally with very little distance between them and a little study shows that vertical grouping would not be much more inconvenient. The lower man would swing through the same distance as the man above him and would therefore be well clear of the upper, longer oar at the end of the stroke, while at the beginning his hands would pass beneath the other oar without hindrance. A very slight staggering of the ports, as in the Victory pediment, would make things still easier and this I think we may well assume from the sculpture, if we feel it necessary. My diagram (Fig. 9) shows an interpretation of the ship in the carving as a trireme with oars of 12, 18 and 24 ft; it may have had two men on one or more of the longer oars without change in the general plan.

There were probably galleys of these two designs among those at Actium, but when that victory had once left the rulers of Rome undisputed masters of the Mediterranean, there was no need to maintain a greater naval force than was required to control piracy; this could be done by small fleets of liburnians based on Naples, Ravenna and Alexandria.

The liburnian had appeared in the Roman fleet a few years before

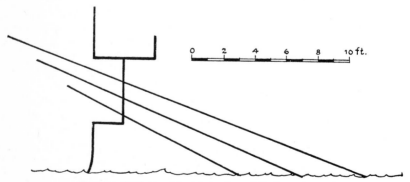

FIG. 9. *Conjectural interpretation of Ostia sculpture*

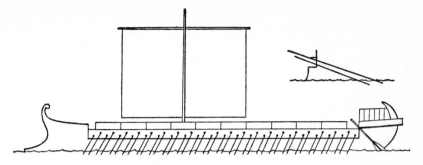

FIG. 10. *Conjectural broadside view of liburnian*

the battle of Actium and it remained the standard fighting ship for some 400 years before being superseded by the dromon. As has been said already, it was a comparatively small two-banked galley and in all probability its oars were carried in the same way as those of the Victory pediment, nearly, but not quite at a single level. Portraits of galleys of this period are rare, but there are two, quite independent, from which we can form a good idea of at least the external appearance of one type.

Frescoes of about A.D. 60 from Pompeii (Plate 6A) show four galleys, three seen from well before the beam and one from the quarter. All have oars in action and one has also a square sail set on a mast stepped well forward. They have definite outriggers and apparently two rows of oars working through them at very nearly the same level, as in the Victory pediment. How many oars there are in each row is hard to say, but an estimate of 15 may not be far wrong.[1] In a mosaic of much the same date (Plate 6B) an almost precisely similar craft is shown with at least 25 oars in the upper row. These galleys, like all others, had practically no sheer except right aft, where the stern rose till it actually curved forward. In the bows the sides were raised, but it is doubtful whether there was any sort of forecastle deck.

My drawing (Fig. 10) shows a broadside view of a galley of this kind with 40 oars a side in two banks, a compromise between the two portraits. She would be about 85 ft long over all with a beam, including the outriggers of about 16 ft.

Galleys of quite another type appear on Trajan's column; they have their oars arranged in a manner reminiscent of the early biremes, Phoenician and Greek, mentioned in Chapter 1. More than one writer has poured scorn on this evidence, but it is confirmed by a piece of sculpture, now in the British Museum, of the same date

[1] See Rodgers, *Naval Warfare under Oars* (1939), Plate 3, or Torr, *Ancient Ships*, Plate 7.

as the column and the frescoes (Plate 7A). In this we see the bow of a galley and the first four pairs of oars, staggered in the old way with the vertical interval between the rows almost the same as that between adjacent oars in the same row. The evidence for superposed banks is undeniable.

It may be that these galleys used by Trajan on the Danube were *triakonters* such as those discussed in Chapter 3, with 15 oars a side. They were certainly *dikrotoi* in the natural sense of having two sets of oars at different levels and, if their predecessors in the days of Alexander the Great were at all similar in design, it is easy to understand their shipping water through the ports for their lower (*kato*) oars. It is also possible, perhaps even probable, that the other type of galley with pairs of oars almost at one level was the liburnian, but neither supposition can be considered proved. All that can be said with confidence is that the Roman fleet in the first century A.D. did contain vessels built on these two very different designs.

The days of the liburnian were those of the final expansion and greatest extent of the Roman empire; during the decline, with the centre of government transferred to Constantinople (or Byzantium), its place was taken by the dromon. Of this type, or at least of its later examples, we know something from written sources, but we have hardly any pictorial evidence to help in their interpretation. The name appears first at the end of the 5th century A.D. and was then used for small craft operating on the waterways at the mouth of the Po. A little later (533) there were 92 dromons in the fleet which Belisarius took to Africa. Rodgers takes contemporary evidence as showing that they had only about 22 oarsmen each,[1] but Torr had already pointed out that the 2,000 men in question were not the normal crews of the dromons, but part of the expeditionary force embarked.[2] These dromons may not have been very large, but they were certainly more than mere 20-oared boats, though their name, derived from the Greek word meaning 'to run,' suggests that they were light handy vessels of some kind.

As has happened since with other names for new types of ship, notably with frigate and clipper, the name dromon came eventually to denote a ship of much greater size and to be used for the largest Byzantine men-of-war, in which, to judge from what little evidence we have, speed and handiness had been sacrificed to fighting power. Unfortunately we have no means of tracing this development of the heavy line-of-battleship dromon from its light predecessor, for it is

[1] *Naval Warfare under Oars*, p. 29.
[2] *Ancient Ships*, p. 17.

not until after A.D. 900 that we have anything to tell us what the fighting ships of Byzantium were like, and even then many questions have to be left unanswered.

In the 10th century the name dromon was used in two senses, both to denote the largest class of all and to cover all ships capable of taking part in close fighting. The name chelandion seems to have been almost its equivalent in the more general sense. In English the term capital ship had at one time a similar double meaning, sometimes denoting any ship fit to lie in the line and sometimes only a First Rate or at least a three-decker.

The Byzantine equivalents of the First Rates, Second Rates and Third Rates of the 18th century were the Dromon, the Pamphylos and the Ousiakos. All had two distinct banks of oars, upper and lower, and the normal number of oars in a bank was 25 on either side; the distinction between the classes lay in the number of men employed on the upper, longer oars. The ousiakos, manned by a single *oussia* or company of 108–110 men, had evidently one man to an oar throughout; the pamphylos of the beginning of the 10th century had a crew of 1½ companies (162–165 men) and must have had two men on each oar in the upper bank; the still larger dromon needed two companies and had 200–230 rowers, not, as one might expect, divided equally between the two banks, but with three men to an oar in the upper bank and the usual one-man oars in the lower.[1]

This threefold classification is no doubt over-simplified, for there were dromons with as many as 120 oars and pamphyloi with as few as 120 rowers. The former must have had 30 oars a side in each bank and the latter 20. Three centuries later and in the western Mediterranean we find that a pamphilus to be built at Genoa was to measure only 30 cubits on the keel.[2] Without going into the difficult question of the exact length of a Genoese cubit it is safe to say that such a vessel can hardly have carried more than 15 or 16 oars in a row. In striking contrast to the usual process the pamphylos seems to have become smaller as time went on.

A smaller type than the ousiakos was called a *moneres* or *galea*. The two names are of interest in themselves, because the first shows that the vessel had a single row of oars and the second is the ancestor of the English word galley and its cousins in other languages. The *galea* had a crew of about 70 and probably rowed about 25 oars a side. It cannot be said for certain that these oars worked on

[1] My description of Byzantine ships is based almost entirely on an article by Mr R. H. Dolley in the *Journal of Roman Studies* for 1948. Where this is not so the mistakes are my own.

[2] Jal, *Glossaire nautique*, s.v. pamphilus.

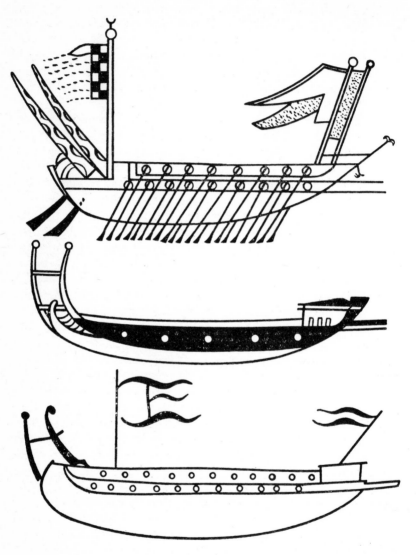

FIG. 11. *Dromons as shown in a manuscript of about* A.D. *1200*

PLATE 5A. Sculpture from Praeneste. *c.* 30 B.C. Vatican Museum

PLATE 5B. Sculpture from Ostia. (Alinari)

PLATE 6A. Wall-painting from Pompeii. (Alinari)

PLATE 6B. Mosaic from Praeneste. (Prof. L. Casson)

PLATE 7A. Roman Liburnian, *c.* A.D. 100. British Museum

PLATE 7B. Dromon, A.D. 1195. Burgerbibliothek, Bern

PLATE 8A. Bronze Door, St Peter's, Rome, *c.* 1430. (Anderson)

PLATE 8B. Graffito from Malaga. Museo Naval, Madrid

an outrigger, but in view of its position as the connecting link between the liburnian and the standard Mediterranean galley of the 15th century this seems more than likely. The outrigger made it possible to carry oars nearer to the ends without making the hull too blunt, and when once that had been realised the device is not likely to have been abandoned and then re-invented.

This point is important, because it has been thought that Byzantine two-banked ships, the dromon, the pamphylos and the ousiakos, were built without outriggers. Casson is very definite on the subject: 'The outrigger had gone with the third bank.'[1] To my mind this is very doubtful; the very few representations of ships of dromon type that have come down to us (Plate 7B and Fig. 11)[2] do seem to suggest that the upper oars at least worked on an outrigger, even if its projection was only slight.

Apparently – one can hardly put it more definitely – dromons were more or less wall sided and blunt-ended. They are said to have had two kinds of ribs, at the ends single pieces rising almost vertically from the keel, amidships first horizontal and then almost vertical, with a right-angle joint. This description must not be taken too literally, because it is obvious that in any form of hull only the extreme end timbers can run anywhere near vertically as a whole, while a right-angle turn at the bilge is not likely in a sea-going vessel intended to use oars. Still, they may have been hard-bilged and full-bodied as compared with the first galleys to which the name dromon was applied, if the apparent derivation of that name goes for anything, though they were still light enough to be beached and some of them could actually be transported over the isthmus of Corinth, as triremes had been before them.

Such a change in shape could be explained by the development of a new weapon to supplement the classical ram. The great polyremes of the Hellenistic period had carried stone-throwing catapults, but now comparatively small vessels had to carry flame-throwers for Greek fire, a liquid whose composition is still uncertain. Large siphons for this purpose were mounted in the bows with smaller weapons of the same kind amidships and aft; the disposition of the armament was in fact very much like that in the later Mediterranean galleys armed with cannon.

The dromon fought under oars, but had masts and sails for making a passage, as was always the case with oared men-of-war.

[1] *The Ancient Mariners*, p. 243.
[2] I have not seen the originals of these drawings, which appear in Landström's recent book *The Ship* and are reproduced with his kind permission, but have full confidence in their accuracy.

How it was rigged is quite uncertain; we cannot be sure how many masts it had or what kind of sail they carried. Two masts seem probable in view of later developments and it is more than probable that the sails were lateens.

The earliest undisputed evidence of the true lateen – the triangular sail with the whole of its leading edge attached to a yard – is to be found in a pair of miniatures in a manuscript of about A.D. 880.[1] A literary reference to the painting of the upper corner of a sail red for purposes of identification dates from the year 533 and has been thought to prove that this was also a lateen, but might equally well apply to most forms of lug or even to a gaff-sail, if such patterns were then in use. As far as we know at present gaff-sails did not appear for another 1,000 years or so, but we used to think much the same about lugs and sprit-sails until quite recently, when Casson discovered representations of both on tombstones not later than A.D. 200.[2]

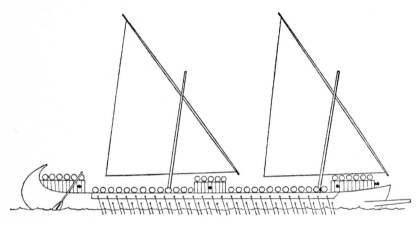

FIG. 12. *Conjectural broadside view of dromon*

At first he claimed that one of these sculptures showed a lateen sail, but examination of the original, as opposed to the copy from which his photograph was taken, proved that the sail was actually a high-pitched lug with a short free luff beneath the fore end of the yard. Such a sail is sometimes called a 'settee' from the type of Mediterranean craft in which it appears.

The relationship of the lug, the settee and the lateen is not at all clear, but it is so close that Moore could write of the settee:

[1] Bibliothèque Nationale, MS.Grec. 510. Reproduced in *The Mariner's Mirror*, 1926, p. 12.
[2] *The Mariner's Mirror*, 1956, pp. 3–5. See also pp. 239–242.

'Had I seen such a sail in the Mediterranean, I should have described it under lateen, and had I seen it in the Hebrides, under lug.'[1] My own preference is for the sequence square sail, lug, lateen, but fresh evidence may well prove me wrong. In any case I believe the dromon of, say, A.D. 500 onwards had high-peaked fore-and-aft sails of some kind.

The Byzantine navy had to face enemies on two sides, Saracens or Arabs from the south and Russians, or rather expatriated Scandinavians, from the north. The northerners came in vessels called by their opponents *monozula*, a word which means literally single pieces of timber. This has been taken to mean that they were simply dug-outs, but it seems most unlikely that fleets of such craft could make the open-sea voyage from the neighbourhood of the Crimea to the Bosphorus. In view of the stage reached by Scandinavian shipbuilders at the time of the first Russian attack on Constantinople in A.D. 865 it is far more probable that they were clinker-built boats of at the very least the standard of the well known Nydam boat and that the name referred to the long one-piece planks of which they were built as contrasted with the shorter planks of a carvel-built hull.

The Arabs, on the other hand, after taking Alexandria with its Imperial dockyard in 640, had built dromons for themselves both there and in Syria. Of these we know very little, but it can be said with some confidence that they were lateen-rigged. Recent discoveries already mentioned show that the lateen or the high-peaked lug was known in the Levant before the arrival of the Arabs, but the very close correspondence between the extreme limits of the Moslem conquest and those of the lateen as the typical sail cannot be ignored. The Arabs may not have invented the lateen; they were certainly responsible for its spread throughout the Mediterranean.

[1] *Last Days of Mast and Sail* (1925), p. 89.

V

English Galleys in the Middle Ages

The question of how a galley can be distinguished from the large open boat which must have been her ancestor was put in the first chapter and answered by making the essential feature the possession of a ram. When we are dealing with Mediterranean waters and with a period some centuries B.C. this is a satisfactory test, but when we move from the Levant to the English Channel and advance in time by some 2,000 years, it fails completely. There were galleys definitely so called in England in the 13th and 14th centuries and these, although built for fighting and propelled by a large number of oars, were certainly not fitted with rams of any kind either above or below the waterline.

The nature of these galleys and of the barges which were their smaller relatives is far from clear, while the disposition of their oars is almost as uncertain as that of the oars of the classical trireme or quinquereme. This is not so much for lack of evidence, since we have inventories and building-accounts in fair quantity, some even giving dimensions. The difficulty is to understand the material at our disposal.

This, apart from a few scraps, consists of the building-accounts for eight out of 20 galleys ordered in 1294 from various sea-port towns, a similar account for the galley *La Phelipe* built in 1336 and an inventory taken in 1373 of the gear of the barge *Paul* whose main dimensions are known from another document. Much of this material has been printed[1] and to some extent interpreted, while

---

[1] Galleys of 1294–6 :—Newcastle, R. J. Whitwell and C. Johnson, *Archaeologia Aeliana*, 1926, and W. R. G. Whitwell, *ibid.*, 1936. Southampton, R. C. Anderson (transcript R. J. Whitwell), *The Mariner's Mirror*, 1928. London, C. Johnson, *The Antiquaries Journal*, 1927. *La Phelipe*, Nicholas, History of the Royal Navy, Vol. 2, app. 2. *Paul*, Riley, Memorials of London — —, 1868, and A. H. Moore, *The Mariner's Mirror*, 1943.

the whole of the evidence has been combined and considered in detail,[1] but it is still by no means clear how these ships were designed and built or how they carried their oars.

We do know that both in rig and in method of construction they were typically 'northern' and entirely different from Mediterranean vessels of the same name. These were lateen-rigged and carvel-built, whereas English galleys, at least in this period, were square-rigged and clinker-built. The second point must be emphasised, because the only study of one of the accounts (Newcastle) by a professional naval architect came to the conclusion that the form of planking must have been double-skin carvel, since the amount of timber provided was far too great for a single thickness. The writer thought it almost impossible to build so large a ship clinker-fashion, but had evidently overlooked the recent discovery that the far larger *Grace Dieu* of 1418 was actually built in what can only be called three-skin clinker, each strake being formed of one 8 in. and two 12 in. planks riveted together, so that at the overlap there were five thicknesses. In all probability some, if not all, of these galleys of 1295 were built in the same way, but with the strakes in two layers instead of three. Certainly they had some form of clinker building, since the accounts mention *clenchatores*, *clynkeres* or *cleyncherers* and *tenences contra clenchatores* or *holderes*. At Newcastle the first of these were called *repercussores*, but in the first entry of their wages this word is followed by *videlicet Clynkers*, so that there is no doubt on the matter even there.

When we come to consider the size of these galleys and the arrangement of their oars, we find little to help us in the one case and still less in the other. All we know is the approximate length of the keel of the Newcastle vessel, or at least its maximum possible length, and the lengths of some of her oars. No other account gives us anything beyond a vague idea of sail-area and probable height of the mast.

The King's orders called for 19 galleys of 120 oars and one, from London, of 140, but how far this programme was carried out is uncertain. We know that the Romney-Hythe galley was never built and that the one from Lyme was very much smaller than she should have been; we also know that London built another of 120 oars, apparently not included in the original programme. As to the others, even where the accounts have survived, it is hard to say how nearly the ships conformed to the standard laid down. On the

[1] J. T. Tinniswood, English Galleys, 1272–1377, *The Mariner's Mirror*, 1949. Gives references to all sources, both manuscript and printed. R. C. Anderson, The Oars of Northern Long-Ships, *ibid.*, 1943.

whole it seems probable that 100 oars was about as many as any
of them could actually row.

The keel of the Newcastle galley was made from two pieces of
timber 52 ft and 58 ft long. We cannot be sure that the full length
of both pieces was used, but it is evident that the keel, allowing for
the scarph, cannot possibly have been more than 105 ft long and
was probably little more than 100 ft. How many oars this galley
rowed is unfortunately somewhat doubtful, but both Ipswich and
Dunwich bought 100 oars for their galleys and it seems fairly certain
that these were no larger than that from Newcastle, if as large.

We are thus faced with the problem of how to fit 50 oars a side
into a ship 100 ft on the keel, and in view of the fact that ancestors
of these long-ships, the Gokstad boat with her 32 oars and the *Long
Serpent* with 68, needed about 3 ft 4 in. of keel for each oar on one
side, this looks at first sight impossible. Still, the *Paul* rowed 80 oars
on an 80-ft keel and this proportion, an oar for every 2 ft of side
above the keel, is just what seems to have been achieved in some,
at least, of these galleys. Canute's great ship of 120 oars must have
been built on some similar plan 200 years before; on the 3 ft 4 in.
standard her length would be incredible.

Any idea of reaching the desired result by reducing the distance
between oar-ports to 2 ft while leaving the rowers in a single line
has to be abandoned at once for obvious reasons based on the size
of an average man. Some kind of bireme design has to be accepted,
but it is not easy to say what kind. It might be something like that
of a classical trireme without the thranite oars and their outrigger,
the oar-ports being staggered at a considerable vertical interval;
on the other hand it might resemble the Mediterranean system *alla
sensile* with two oars close together at the same level, the shorter
forward and their two rowers side by side.

All that we have to help us is the knowledge that the Newcastle
galley had some oars of 22 or 23 ft and some of 16 or 17 ft besides
others of unspecified length. This suggests pairs of oars differing by
6 ft over all or about 2 ft inboard, enough to let the two rowers sit
or stand more or less side by side in comfort, but not enough for
any arrangement in which the longer oar was carried at a much
greater height above the water than the other.

This in turn points to something very like the *alla sensile* system
or the much older arrangement shown on the Victory pediment,
where two oar-ports actually overlap, with the foremost *very* slightly
lower than the aftermost. It has been objected that both these
arrangements were essentially southern and always used in galleys
with a parallel-sided outrigger or *apostis*, built in an entirely different

way from their English namesakes; while this style of rowing, with oars almost touching one another, demanded greater skill than could be expected of scratch crews such as were often employed in England. There is also the question whether there was at this date enough intercourse between the Mediterranean and the Channel to explain the adoption by English shipbuilders of even a much modified version of a southern design.

Bayonne, then a part of Edward I's realm, has been suggested as a possible link between north and south, but that link seems to have been stronger in a northerly direction than a southerly; for although the evidence is very scanty, what little there is – largely negative – points to clinker-building there as in England. There was a proposal in 1276 to build galleys of 120, 100 and 80 oars at Bayonne and English-built galleys were sometimes repaired and refitted there, but there is no suggestion that the local manner of building was in any way different from that used in England. It is also probable that the very large ship under construction there in 1419 was clinker-built in the same way as her English contemporary the *Grace Dieu*, mentioned above. The letter describing her progress speaks of her as being '36 strakes in height boarded' with 11 beams in place,[1] whereas for a carvel-built ship one would expect to read that she was 'all framed up' with planking under way, or something of that sort. This again is mainly negative evidence, but it does tend to show that the shipbuilders of Bayonne were still building clinker-fashion more than a century after the time of the galleys now being considered.[2]

A far more likely link can be found much nearer home than Bayonne, for the French had a fleet of galleys based on the Seine and these were certainly of Mediterranean type. 'Whenever galleys had to be built or repaired, southern workmen, who understood flush-jointed building, had to be brought at great expense from Genoa, Marseilles, etc.'[3] Southern carvel-built galleys must have carried their oars in southern fashion and this would then be known on the other side of the Channel and might well be copied as far as it could be in northern hulls.

The difficulty of rowing may not have been so great as has been supposed. An allowance of 2 ft of side to each oar means that pairs would be separated by intervals of 4 ft centre to centre. This is more than the Venetian standard; there, groups of three were

[1] The full text is printed in *The Mariner's Mirror*, 1922, p. 376.
[2] It is only fair to mention that Laughton in an unpublished note took this same sentence as proof of carvel-building.
[3] De la Ronciere, *Histoire de la Marine française*, Vol., p. 407.

placed less than 3 ft 9 in. apart (3¼ ft V.) and biremes would have needed even less. Certainly with a 4-ft spacing there would be no need to put the shorter oar so near the longer as was done in the Mediterranean.

The conclusion is then that the galleys of Ipswich, Dunwich, Newcastle and York (where 97 oars are recorded) were 100 ft or a trifle more on the keel and had their oars disposed in pairs at one level, the pairs being about 4 ft apart. Those built in London were probably built on the same pattern, but were larger, perhaps 120 ft and 140 ft on the keel.

Two from the south coast, those of Southampton and Lyme, have to be considered separately. The first, judging by cost and number of man-days required for building, must have been about as large as those from the east coast ports, but her account mentions only 60 oars. If this was indeed her full complement, they could have been carried singly on the old 3 ft 4 in. spacing; while by having oars long enough to be pulled by two men the builders might reasonably claim that she was at least equivalent to a galley with 120 one-man oars. Lyme built a much smaller craft, not more than about 75 ft on the keel by the same method of calculation, and bought 54 oars for her. This number is too small for pairs at 4-ft intervals and too large for single oars normally spaced. Failing new evidence, which is most unlikely, her design must remain a mystery.

A strange feature about all these accounts is that they contain no mention of oar-ports, rowlocks or thole-pins and none of thwarts for the rowers. The Newcastle document does indeed record the purchase of timber *ad scalmas* and these were at first taken to be thole-pins, although the Latin word for these should be *scalmos*, but have since been shown to be curved pieces forming the built-up stems.

Such lack of written evidence – pictorial there is none – prevents complete certainty whether the oars were worked over the gunwale or through holes lower down, but the latter is by far the more likely. Even comparatively small craft such as the Gokstad and Oseberg boats had oar-ports as far back as 900 and the Bayeux tapestry, dating from 1100 or so, shows the same thing. It is also recorded that three ships built in Norway in 1206 had two rows of oar-ports amidships, a thing not known there either before or afterwards.[1] The emphasis is clearly not on the mere presence of ports, but on there having been two rows of them.

In these ships there were 24 oars on either side in the upper row and 12 in the lower, the longest oars measuring 20 ells. Unfortu-

[1] *Nikolaysen Langskibet fra Gokstad*, 1882, p. 29.

nately authorities differ as to the length of an ell in Norway at this time. Nikolaysen gives the information in the form '20 (now 15) ells (9.41 m.)' and in various other places makes the new ell .647 m., as it had been before the adoption of the metric system, and the old ell ¾ of that or .47 m.; while Brögger uses the value .55 m. without indicating his reason for doing so.[1] One therefore makes the oars 31 ft long, the other 36 ft. This matter of what an ell measured will have to be considered again in connection with the question of the sail area carried by these northern long-ships.

First it will be as well to say a little more about their hulls. They were double-ended with a curved stem aft as well as forward. The problem of attaching a straight sternpost to the keel, to carry the recently introduced median rudder, had been solved at least 50 years earlier, but in these ships, or some of them, it was dodged by fitting a sort of deadwood on the after stem and hanging the rudder on that. At the same time the old-fashioned side rudder was kept as an alternative or an auxiliary.

How long the rakes were and what proportion the length over all bore to that on the keel can only be guessed. A western balinger of about 1400 had rakes totalling slightly more than one-third of the keel,[2] while the proportion in the big ship of Bayonne was as much as two-thirds. Both of these had straight sternposts and one might well expect a double-ender to reach at least the second figure, but perhaps ½ K. will be a reasonable allowance. This would make a galley of 100 ft on the keel 150 ft over all, with rakes at each end equal to the beam, that being 25 ft on the known proportions of the *Paul*.

Light castles were built at each end and a row of hurdles, perhaps double, ran fore-and-aft between these above the gunwale as a protection for the rowers against an enemy's missiles and to some extent from the weather. In this, English medieval galleys showed some resemblance to their *kataphract* ancestors of classical times. Of their internal arrangements or even their deck-plan we know nothing; it is not even certain that they had a true deck at all. Quite probably the spaces between the beams were simply covered by the hatches, of which there is frequent mention, and these were no doubt easily removed.

Calculations as to sail plan depend largely on figures recorded for *La Phelipe* taken in conjunction with the *Paul*, which rowed the same number of oars and whose dimensions are known. These were 80 ft keel and 20 ft beam; but there can be very little doubt that

[1] Brögger and Shetelig, *The Viking Ships*, 1953, p. 193.
[2] *The Mariner's Mirror*, 1945, p. 165. From a Venetian MS.

La Phelipe was a good deal larger. Estimates of her size based on cube roots of cost or man-days needed for building, or on square roots of the amount of canvas needed for sails, all lead to the conclusion that she was at least 10 per cent longer than the galleys of Newcastle, Ipswich and Dunwich and probably more. The *Paul*, with 80 oars on an 80-ft keel must have been built on the bireme plan with 2 ft of side to each oar, but *La Phelipe* was too large for this. It would seem that she must have carried her oars singly in the old fashion; they may perhaps have been very slightly closer together than usual and extended rather farther towards the ends. As an alternative it may be that she was longer in comparison with her beam than earlier galleys and so longer than would be expected from the calculations just mentioned. If so, the same may have been true of the Lyme galley, in which the number of oars bore exactly the same awkward relation to the estimated keel-length.

La Phelipe had a sail 25 ells deep and 26 cloths wide. If we knew the value of an ell and the width of a cloth, all would be well, but both of these are uncertain. Laughton assumed that an ell was the same as a modern yard and that a cloth was ¾ yard wide, and on that basis made her sail measure 75 ft by 54 ft and her mast 95 ft.[1] His views always deserved respect, but to me so large a sail seemed out of place in a shallow hull not likely to have been more than 25 ft in beam. In this I had the support of a professional seaman, Captain Verwey, both of us suggesting that an ell was more probably 2 ft and the sail therefore 50 ft deep with a mast of about 62 ft.[2] For the width of a cloth Verwey preferred 18 in. and it is worth noting that the normal width towards the end of the 18th century was 24 in. as against Laughton's 27 in.

The *New English Dictionary* defines an ell very vaguely as a measure varying in different countries and specifies an English ell of 45 in., a Scottish of 37½ in. and a Flemish of 27 in.; it does not suggest that an ell was at any time or in any country equal to 3 ft. Etymologically speaking, an ell should be the same as a cubit, 18 in. or half a yard, and that is evidently what Nikolaysen believed the Norwegian ell to have been in 1206 and earlier, his more modern ell being 2 ft. Such a 2-ft ell was at one time almost universal in Scandinavia and Germany, the exact length depending on that of the local foot. It will probably be admitted that any value greater than 3 ft would make *La Phelipe's* sail impossibly large; the Flemish ell of 27 in. is a possibility and a simple 2 ft at least worth consideration.

[1] *The Mariner's Mirror*, 1929, p. 76.
[2] *Ibid.*, 1931, p. 286.

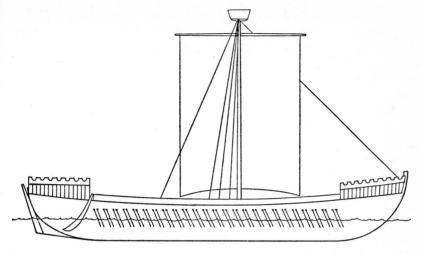

FIG. 13. *Conjectural broadside view of English galley of 1300*

Some indication of sail-plan can be got from the lengths of standing rigging, when these are known. The depth of a sail must obviously be less than that of the shrouds supporting the mast, because they started well above its head and came down at an angle to a point at least level with its foot. Roughly speaking the shortest possible shroud in the diagram given by Laughton for his 75-ft sail would have an effective length of at least 80 ft without any allowance for whatever method of making fast and setting up was in use in those days. A backstay must have been longer by an amount depending on how far aft it led.

We have no figures for any part of *La Phelipe*'s rigging, but we do know that the larger of the two London galleys had backstays of 23[1] and 20 'teys'. Assuming that these were fathoms (French *toise*) we have 138 and 120 ft; while a calculation based on the amount of material needed for these and for her 16 shrouds shows that, if the shrouds were of the same thickness as the backstays, their average length was 100 ft. Using the square roots of the total amount of canvas required for the sails we find that *La Phelipe*'s rigging ought to measure roughly $\frac{5}{6}$ of the London galley's. This would give her backstays of 115 and 100 ft and shrouds averaging 83 ft; by the same reckoning the figures for the Dunwich galley with her 800 ells of canvas would be about 105, 90 and 75 ft.

The length of 83 ft obtained by this calculation for *La Phelipe*'s

---

[1] The transcript given by Johnson (*op. cit.*, p. 434, last line) gives 'xxiiii', but I have it on his authority that this was a misprint or misreading for 'xxiii.'

shrouds agrees so well with the 80 ft minimum given above as taken
from Laughton's diagram with its 75-ft sail that there can be very
little doubt that he was right in taking an ell as the same as a yard
and Captain Verwey and I wrong in preferring one of 2 ft.[1] The
matter can be made even more certain by a reference to the account
for refitting a galley at Winchelsea in 1347. This was a contemporary
of *La Phelipe* and seems also to have had 80 oars. Her 18 shrouds
measured 14 'tes' each and her backstays 15; the measure is
evidently the same as the London 'teys' and so a fathom. The
shrouds were thus 84 ft long and the backstays 90 ft. Given that a
fathom was 6 ft there is no denying that an ell must have been 3 ft.

That being so, we have to accept a 75-ft sail and a 95-ft mast
for *La Phelipe* with about 65 and 85 as the figures for the 100-oared
galleys of 1295 and at least 90 and 115 as those for the larger galley
from London. The *Paul* on the same standard would have had a
sail rather more than 50 ft deep and a mast of nearly 70 ft. These
masts had small top-castles carried before the mast. They were
supported in the normal way by shrouds, stays (called forestays)
and backstays.

Bowsprits were not always present and were quite small in any
case; the luff seems to have been a more important fitting, but its
exact nature is still uncertain, though it is believed to have served
to spread the tack of the sail. The yard was hoisted by ties and
controlled by lifts and yard-ropes or braces; the sail had sheets
with no mention of separate tacks and there were a number of
other running ropes whose nature is not yet clear. Some of the
earlier accounts mention a single bowline, but it is by no means
certain that this had anything to do with the sail; it and the bowsprit may have belonged to the anchor-gear. On the other hand
the *Paul's* two bowlines do seem likely to have helped to set the
sail in the same way as those of later years.

It is fortunate that enough material has been preserved to give
us at least a sketchy idea of what these English 14th-century
galleys were like, since they are the last descendants of the Viking
long-ship of which we can say anything of the sort. The balingers
of the 15th century were no doubt clinker-built square-rigged ships
which could also use oars, but we know so little about them that
it is useless to do more than note that there were such ships and
that they probably belonged to the same family.

---

[1] There was a silly mistake in my reckoning; I halved the length of the London
backstays before starting my calculations, either thinking of them as put on double or
perhaps merely dividing by two because a ship has two sides. Why no one called attention
to this is a mystery.

Whatever the balinger was like, her rise seems to have been accompanied by a change in the meaning of the word galley as applied to an English fighting ship, for the galley *Jesu Maria* described in accounts of 1410–11 as recently built or rebuilt (*de novo fact'*), not as a foreign prize or purchase, was certainly southern in design. She had a yard formed of two pieces, she had her shrouds set up by blocks and she had no fewer than 240 oars weighted with lead. Even as a trireme – and there is no evidence that southern builders had yet gone farther than that with grouped oars – she must have been a very long vessel and very difficult for an untrained crew to manage. This may explain why she disappears almost at once and why we find no further mention of galleys in England until the appearance of another single example late in the reign of Henry VIII.

VI

Southern Galleys Alla Sensile

From the end of the 13th century to the end of the 18th, when it disappeared from the scene, the standard fighting galley of the Mediterranean remained almost unchanged in design except for one very important feature, the disposition of the rowers. Not so much that of the oars themselves, for they continued to be worked at one level on a projecting outrigger; but, whereas in the 14th and 15th centuries they were arranged in groups of three with one man on each, these groups were replaced before the middle of the 16th century by single oars worked by several men, usually five, but sometimes as many as seven.

The earlier system, with which this chapter is concerned, was called *alla sensile*, with the usual variations in spelling. The meaning is 'in the simple fashion' and to the extent that each oar was worked in the simplest possible fashion by a single man the description is adequate, but the arrangement of the oars in groups of three with less than 10 in. (English) between their tholes and the groups only about 3 ft 8 in. apart, centre to centre, was very far from the simplicity of its successor.

These Mediterranean triremes are said on good authority to have appeared first at the end of the 13th century and to have been developed from biremes built on the same system.[1] The new type was soon well established; it is certain that galleys with three men to a bank were in general use by the middle of the 14th century. We know, for instance that in 1354 the galleys of Barcelona were rowed by 180 or 174 men[2] and that can only mean that they had 30 or 29 banks with oars in groups of three.

[1] Sanudo, *Liber Secretorum* — —, Hanover, 1611; written about 1320. 'It must be known that in A.D. 1290 in nearly all galleys two men rowed on the same bank. Soon more ingenious men recognised that three men could row on each of them. Nearly everyone uses this method now.'

[2] Bofarull, *Antigua Marina Catalana* (1898), pp. 11–13.

Unfortunately we have no contemporary representations of these early biremes from which the medieval trireme was developed. The nearest approach to such a thing is in a fresco at Siena showing a 13th-century battle, but this is work of about 1400 and it should be mentioned that the battle depicted, that of Cape Salvore, was probably imaginary. In the case of a similar vessel shown on a map of as late as 1482 the artist seems to have drawn a *fusta*, the galley's smaller sister; these we know had their oars sometimes in twos and sometimes in threes.

Some Spanish drawings of the latter part of the 13th century show biremes of an entirely different kind with their oars as obviously at two levels as those of the Phoenician ships of 700 B.C. These drawings cannot be ignored, but their value as evidence is doubtful, since they show vessels far more like sailing ships than galleys in shape and strongly suggest copying from some source or sources not properly understood by the artist, perhaps a combination of a Spanish sailing ship and a Byzantine dromon. A map of a century later (1375) shows a Catalonian *uxer* with a hull of very different shape quite like that of a normal galley and, though we know very little about this type, we do know that it belonged to the galley family. The vessel is under sail and no oars are shown, but there is no doubt about the outrigger.[1]

The idea that the other Spanish artist was influenced by what he knew of a dromon is strengthened by a comparison of his ships with that shown in Plate 7B which must, from its date and subject, have been at least meant for a dromon. The same is probably true of the galley shown on the bronze door of St Peter's (Plate 8A). This is also a Byzantine galley on the way to Italy, but is work of as late as 1445; if it is anything like a true portrait, either the artist or the Byzantines must have been very much behind the times, for by then the one-level trireme had been well established for more than a century. To tell the truth this galley is difficult to explain. Its hull is very like that of a merchant-galley in a Venetian manuscript of just the same date,[2] but its oars, instead of being grouped in threes at one level, are shown in pairs with one oar of each working on the outrigger and the other beneath it. Certainly this is more suggestive of a dromon than of any other type.

On the other hand the galley in Plate 8B from a *graffito* found at Malaga and believed to be Moorish work of the end of the 14th century appears to have a single row of oars at regular intervals.

---

[1] See Artiñano, *Arquitectura Naval Española*, Plate 7 for the 'biremes' and p. 20 for the *uxer*.

[2] Reproduced in *The Mariner's Mirror*, 1925, p. 144.

If it were not for the presence of side-rudders without a stern-rudder it might be taken for at least 150 years later. These two galleys are puzzles and will probably remain so.

It is very hard to say whether these medieval biremes and triremes with their oars in groups at one level were direct descendants of similar galleys in classical times. Those who believe that the Athenian trireme had its oars arranged in the same way as its Venetian namesake of some 1,800 years later will have no difficulty in believing that the design had never quite disappeared; but those whose idea of the Greek trireme is very different will be more than doubtful. Comparatively small craft with a single row of oars about 3½ ft apart have no doubt existed ever since oars were first evolved from paddles, but the close pairing of oars at one level probably had to be invented afresh. When that happened is impossible to say; my own guess would be somewhere between A.D. 1000 and 1200, but I may well be entirely wrong.

With the establishment of the new trireme as the standard type of fighting galley we at last reach firm ground. A model of a sailing ship of the first half of the 15th century, especially a 'northerner', would have to be based to a great extent on guess-work, but in the case of a galley it would be possible to produce contemporary evidence for nearly every detail. The fact that most of that evidence comes from Venice is not important, for it is certain that the *galia sottil*, the light, fighting galley differed very little from one Mediterranean fleet to another.

Its carvel-built hull was long and narrow, with hardly any sheer except right aft. Roughly speaking, its length without the projecting beak and the overhanging poop was at least eight times the beam of the true hull and the depth little more than a third of the beam. A little above the deck-level, with its sides supported by rising extensions of the beams, came the long rectangular *telaro*, a frame carrying the thole-pins. This was shorter than the true hull by an amount about equal to the beam and was placed slightly nearer to the stem than to the sternpost. Its width was about 1⅓ times the beam, so that it projected by 2 ft or more on either side, even amidships. The width of its after end might be a trifle less than that forward.

The groups of thole-pins were distributed along its two sides in the manner already described, about 44 in. centre to centre with 10 in. between adjacent tholes of a group. The rowers' benches were not strictly speaking thwarts, since they did not run continuously from side to side, but were in two parts separated by a narrow fore-and-aft gangway, the *corsia*, and reached only about

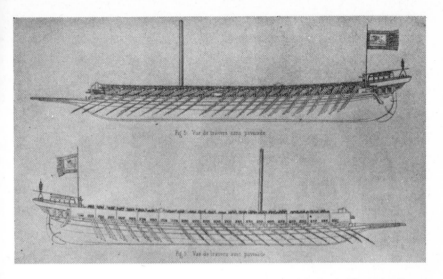

PLATE 9A. Venetian trireme, 1539. Model by Admiral Fincati. From
Souvenirs de Marine, Vol. 2

PLATE 9B. Spanish galleys off Tunis, 1535. Spanish Royal Tapestries

PLATE 10A. The galeass *Bull*, 1546

PLATE 10B. The galley *Subtylle*, 1543
Drawings by Anthony Anthony. British Museum

PLATE 11A. Turkish galley, *c.* 1680. From Witsen, *XXX Platen van vreemde Vaartuigen*

PLATE 11B. French galley, *c.* 1690. From *Neptune François*

PLATE 12A. Maltese galley, *c.* 1775. Water-colour in author's collection

PLATE 12B. Half-galley, *c.* 1800. From Baugean, *Collection de toutes les espéces de Batimens*

half way from there to the edge of the *telaro*. They ran at an angle with their inner ends about a foot farther aft than the outer, thus letting the man on the aftermost and longest oar of a group sit slightly farther aft than his neighbour, an arrangement obviously made necessary by the position of their respective thole-pins.

Inboard, the oars differed in length by an amount just enough to let their rowers work efficiently side by side, something between 18 in. and 2 ft. Normally an oar has about a third of its length inboard and two-thirds outboard, and if the leverage was to be kept the same, this would have entailed a difference of at least 3 ft outboard and some 5 ft in total length. Actually the difference was much less. A list of oars in store in the Arsenal of Venice in 1544 shows that the great majority of those classed as *pianeri, postizi* and *terzicci* – the names for the three oars of a group – were of three lengths, 30½, 28½ and 26½ ft (Venetian).[1] This difference (27 in. English) was not very much more than would be needed inboard and cannot have allowed the length outboard to differ by much more than 1 ft.

In a treatise of almost the same date (1539) Cristoforo Canale, a Venetian flag officer, mentioned the fact that some people liked to have all the oars of the same length outboard and some thought otherwise. He expressed his own preference for the 'unequal' arrangement, but at the same time gave a bird's-eye view of a galley showing the most perfect equality. In any case, with the lengths he gives for the oars, 32, 30½ and 29½ ft, the difference outboard must have been barely noticeable.[2]

One thing is certain; the shorter oars had the larger fraction of their length outboard; in other words, the three rowers worked with three different leverages. At first sight this appears a thoroughly bad arrangement, but closer consideration suggests that there were compensations. The three oars had to travel through the same angle to avoid fouling one another and this meant that the length of stroke differed, the handle of the longest oar having to be moved through the greatest distance. At the same time, though, its greater length inboard meant that there was less leverage to overcome, so that an increase in the length of stroke was balanced by a decrease in the effort needed to make it. This explanation may have its faults from the mechanical point of view, but there can be no doubt that the trireme system worked; otherwise it would not have lasted for some 250 years unchanged.

The Venetian galley *alla sensile* went very near to forming an

---

[1] Fincati, *Le Triremi* (1881), p. 22.
[2] *Ibid.*, pp. 19, 20 and 80.

exception to the almost universal rule that any type of fighting ship grows in size as time goes on. English sailing two-deckers, for instance, grew by at least 15 per cent in both length and beam in the course of the 18th century; while at Venice in more than twice that length of time the dimensions of galleys increased by no more than $3\frac{1}{2}$ per cent. It was not until after the introduction of a new method of rowing that any great increase in size took place.

This point is best shown by a comparison of figures given by three writers roughly a century apart in date. They have been converted to English measure from Venetian paces and feet, the Venetian foot being roughly equal to $13\frac{5}{8}$ in. English and a pace containing five feet of 16 inches.

	Sanudo (*c.* 1320)	Timbotta (*c.* 1440)	Canale (1539)
Length, stem to sternpost ...	132 ft	134 ft	137 ft
Beam, hull only ...	$16\frac{1}{2}$ ft	16 ft	$17\frac{1}{8}$ ft

These figures refer to the general run of fighting galleys, but there were others of greater size used by flag officers, just as there were ships of 100 guns or more when the ordinary ship-of-the-line was a 74. At the end of the *alla sensile* period such flagships had reached a length of $152\frac{1}{2}$ ft and a beam of 18 ft. They might have as many as 30 banks or groups of oars on either side, whereas the ordinary galley had 25.

Some at least of these larger galleys were quadriremes with oars in groups of four and there was one quinquereme on the same system, built at Venice by Vettor Fausto in 1529. It seems, however, that a galley with oars in pairs and two men on each could also be called a quadrireme and that such a vessel had been built at Genoa in 1535 to serve as the flagship of Charles V in his expedition to Tunis. According to Duro[1] she had 26 banks and rowed four oars on each, so that – omitting two banks for the cook-house and the boat – she was propelled by 190 oars. The total should be 192, but that is not the point; the fact is that in the contemporary wall paintings in the Alhambra of Granada the number of oars shown on one side of this flag-galley is not 96 but about half that number (Fig. 14). The state of the painting, disfigured by the vandalism of name-scratchers as well as the passage of time, prevents exact counting, but 45 is the minimum and there may be two or three more.[2] As a quadrireme there must have been the normal four men

[1] *Armada Española*, Vol. 1, p. 222. He gives no authority.
[2] My drawing (full size) was made in 1918. Very probably the painting has deteriorated since then.

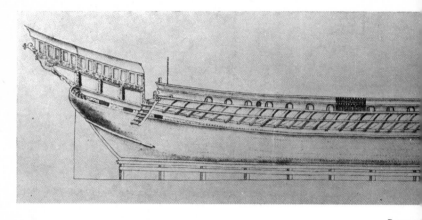

PLATE 13

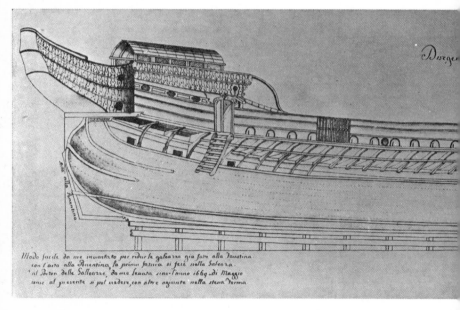

Disege

*Modo facile da me inuentato per ridurle galeazze gia fare alla Faustina
con l'asta alla Ponentina, fo primo fatura si fece nella Sateoza
al Porton delle Gallcazze, da me lenata sino l'anno 1669 di Maggio
come al presente si pol vedere con altre agiunte nella stessa forma*

PLATE 13B. Venetian galeass, 1686.

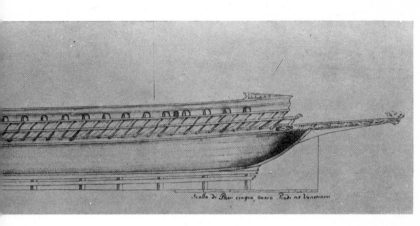

galley, 1686

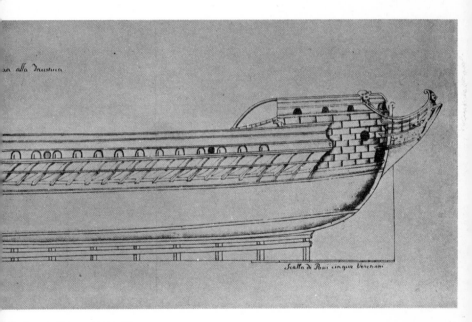

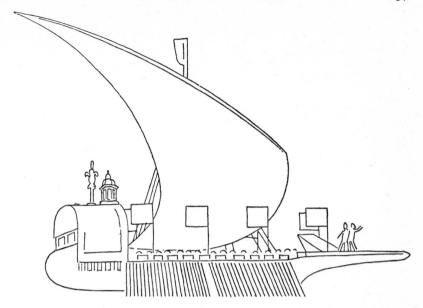

FIG. 14. *Spanish Flag-galley off Tunis, 1535. From the Alhambra*

to a bank, but they must have been employed on two oars instead of four.[1]

Although the design of Fausto's quinquereme was never repeated, she deserves a little consideration as marking the final development of the galley *alla sensile*. She was 158 ft long (28 paces Venetian) and must have been about 20 ft wide, not counting the outrigger; she drew 5 ft 8 in. as against the 4 ft 6 in. of an ordinary light galley and had twice as many oars. Here Casoni in his *Dei Navigli Poliremi* (1838) made the most incomprehensible mistake. In his own words: 'Remembering that the *galea sottile* of the 15th century had 45 oars, as did that of the 17th century, the quinquereme must have had 90, that is to say 45 a side, and these grouped in fives would make nine banks. Actually a normal light galley had 25 banks with three oars a side on each, 150 oars in all; the quinquereme would therefore have had 300 oars in groups of five, or 30 banks.'[2]

---

[1] Guglielmotti, *Storia della Marina Pontificia*, Vol. 3, p. 409, describes the same galley as having 30 banks and 60 oars each worked by 6 men (in the later *al scaloccio* fashion). He offers no explanation of the fact that a contemporary authority, whom he quotes, calls her a 'quadrireme'.

[2] I have ignored the fact that a space equivalent to 1 bank or perhaps 2 was occupied on one side by the boat and on the other by the cook-room, because I am not sure whether these spaces were always included in the number of banks. When comparing one type with another this makes little difference.

The strange thing is that, working from a series of false assumptions, he managed to reach a result not far from the truth in reckoning the probable length of the quinquereme at 153½ ft. Jal, with the same statement as to the relative number of oars in a trireme and a quinquereme as his guide, put the length at 254 ft and commented: 'Quelle gigantesque galère!'[1]

The first reports on Fausto's quinquereme were moderately enthusiastic, but no more were built and the original was laid up after a few months' service. She was certainly still in existence in 1551[2] and according to one account was the flagship of Marcantonio Colonna as Commander in Chief of the Christian fleet and commander of the Papal squadron in 1570, that squadron consisting of 12 galleys lent by Venice to the Pope and manned and equipped at his expense. If so, she was destroyed by lightning in December of that year. Other accounts make Colonna's galley a quadrireme, but still speak of Fausto as her builder.[3] In any case, by 1570 the change to single oars each worked by several men had been made and she would then have been neither a quinquereme nor a quadrireme in the old sense.

We have two scraps of information about the quinquereme's armament. She was given 100 arquebuses as compared with 50 for a light galley, where the allowance seems to have been one for each group of oars on either side, and she carried *triginta tormenta bellica*. At an earlier date these 30 *tormenta* would have been catapults or other mechanical weapons, but by the 16th century they must have been guns. Greek fire was no longer in use and even its composition seems to have been forgotten.

Guns of a sort had appeared afloat before the middle of the 14th century. The date 1354 often given for the invention of gunpowder is certainly too late, for there is evidence of its use in primitive guns ashore at least 30 years earlier and it is known that a gun was carried aboard an English ship in 1337.[4] In spite of this it is very doubtful whether galleys carried anything more than mere hand-weapons for another 100 years. Venetian manuscripts of the first half of the 15th century describe the design and construction

---

[1] *Archéologie navale*, Vol. 1, p. 389.

[2] Jal, p. 390. Fincati, *Le Trireme*, p. 56, puts her last appearance in the inventories in 1544.

[3] Casoni, p. 35, quotes a contemporary reference to the destruction of 'la galia quinquereme dove sopra v'era il general del papa Marcantonio Colonna'. Guglielmotti, *Marcantonio Colonna alla Battaglia di Lepanto*, gives part of a letter saying that his flagship was 'una galea quadrireme del Fausto' which had not been to sea for 30 years.

[4] Guglielmotti, *Storia della Pontificia*, Vol. 2, pp. 27–51, and *The Mariner's Mirror*, 1960, p. 70.

of galleys in great detail[1] without mentioning guns at all and pictures afford similar negative evidence. For my part I should be surprised to find proof of the presence of real guns in galleys before 1450 and even that date may be too early.

When they did come into use, it was inevitable that they should be for the most part carried right forward and should fire in that direction. For 2,000 years or more, naval tactics in the Mediterranean had been based on the use of the ram and therefore of attacking the enemy end-on. A gun firing forward became an extension of the ram and made it possible to inflict damage on the enemy without, or at least before, coming into actual contact.

The strange thing is that the true ram, striking at or near the waterline, had been replaced by a comparatively fragile beak well above the water long before the gun appeared to take its place. How long before we can only guess. It would seem that the galleys from Marseilles with which Richard I sank a very large Saracen dromon – probably a sailing ship – in 1191 must have been of the older type, since it is hard to believe that mere above-water beaks could have done this without leaving the galleys too badly damaged for further service. On the other hand the dromons of about the same date shown in Plates 7B and 8A and Fig. 11 seem to have the new form of bow with a beak rather than a ram. The change may have come towards the end of the 12th century, but it may equally well have begun a good deal earlier.

It is safe to assume that the heavy gun, a bombard, was carried right forward in a fixed carriage and fired over the beak with no means of training or even elevation. Towards the end of the *alla sensile* period it was flanked by two pairs of smaller guns on swivel mountings, the heavier pair amidships and the lighter outboard. A similar arrangement lasted for the rest of the life of the Mediterranean galley and had probably come into use as soon as guns became common.

At the other end of the ship there came a drastic change in the steering gear, the replacement of the two side-rudders of classical times by a single rudder hung on the sternpost. The new type of rudder is believed to have appeared first in the Netherlands or on the southern shores of the Baltic about the beginning of the 13th century; before that northern clinker-built ships had carried rudders on the starboard quarter. To judge from the name given by the Venetians to the sternpost rudder, *timon bavonescho*, it may have reached the Mediterranean from Bayonne together with the

---

[1] Jal, *Archéologie navale*, Vol. 2, pp. 6–30; *The Mariner's Mirror*, 1925, pp. 135–165, and 1945, pp. 160–167.

northern one-masted square rig, said to have been introduced by pirates from that port in 1303.

At first both kinds of rudder were carried. A Catalan *uxer* of 1354 had two *timon* and one *govern*[1] and a rough sketch in the early 15th-century Venetian manuscript known as *Fabbrica di galere* shows a galley with the two kinds of rudder very clearly.[2] Another drawing from the middle of the century shows the stern rudder only[3] and it may be that the change was complete by then, but it must be noted that this is a long-voyage merchant galley and that those meant for fighting may have kept the side rudders longer. Still, in spite of the difficulty of hanging it on a curved sternpost, the stern rudder had ousted those on the quarters well before 1500.

There remains the matter of rig. It is hardly necessary to say that the sails were lateens and that this remained the case as long as the Mediterranean galley lasted, and yet it seems strange that this should have been so. The lateen's strong point is in windward work and it is hard to believe that so narrow and shallow a vessel as a galley ever attempted to sail to windward at all. Her sailing must always have been well off the wind and for that a square sail would have been more suitable. However, lateens were the only sails of the Mediterranean when the trireme *alla sensile* was introduced and conservatism or perhaps some other factor not now obvious ensured their survival.

Venetian galleys had one mast stepped about $\frac{1}{3}$ or $\frac{3}{10}$ of the length from the stem. According to one authority 'the Provençal and Genoese had two and these, with the Catalan, — — were better under sail, but were inferior to the Venetians under oars.'[4] This statement is confirmed to some extent by the fact that the Catalan inventory already mentioned lists an *abre maior* and an *abre del mig* (a mizzen mast), but the great majority of 14th and 15th-century representations of galleys show only one mast, whatever their nationality. A very small square sail set right forward does appear occasionally, but this was probably more or less a 'lash up' for use in emergency, no more a part of the working rig than its ancestor the Greek *akateion*.

---

[1] Inventory printed by Bofarull, *Antigua Marina Catalana* (1898), pp. 11–13.
[2] Lane, *Venetian Ships and Shipbuilders* (1934), p. 12.
[3] Lane, p. 23 or *The Mariner's Mirror*, 1925, p. 144.
[4] D'Albertis, *Le Costruzione Navali — — al tempo di — Colombo* (1893), pp. 25–6.

VII

Henry VIII's Oared Men-of-War

The word galeass in its native Italian form *galeazza* was originally no more than an alternative name for the *galera grossa* or great galley used by the Venetians for trading voyages both eastwards in the Mediterranean and westwards to the ports of England and Flanders; it was not until the latter part of the 16th century that it began to be used in southern Europe for a heavy oared vessel intended for fighting. Great galleys had indeed been present at the 'deplorable battle of Zonchio' in 1499, but these must have been ordinary merchant-galleys with a few extra guns and an increased crew. The galeasses of Lepanto (1571) seem to have been the first built, or perhaps converted, with fighting as their primary object.

These Mediterranean galeasses were meant to combine the freedom of movement of the galley with the seaworthiness and something of the fighting power of the sailing man-of-war. In both respects they were unsatisfactory; they could neither keep up with galleys under oars nor with normal sailing ships under sail. Still, in spite of their faults, they remained a feature of, at least, Venetian fleets for some 150 years.

In quite another theatre vessels combining the square rig and broadside armament of the sailing ship with the oars of the galley had appeared some years earlier and some of them had actually been called galeasses, though the name had also been applied to an ill-defined class of moderate-sized ships without oars.

The first of these oared galeasses were built in England in 1546, but as far back as 1515 Henry VIII's *Great Galley* had been an outstanding example of the same combination of oars and sails and the close of the previous century had seen at least two ships, the *Sweepstake* and *Mary Fortune* of similar type, though much smaller. Henry VIII built also two classes of smaller oared men-of-war, pinnaces and rowbarges, and though neither these nor his galeasses remained long in use, his attempts to produce satisfactory hybrids between the sailing ship and the galley deserve as full a description as can be based on the very scanty evidence available.

The *Great Galley* was a remarkable ship, even more remarkable than the far better known *Henry Grace a Dieu*, for that ship was only a slight advance on previous patterns, whereas the *Great Galley* represented an enormous stride, too great for the technical possibilities of her time. Clinker-built at first and probably the last big ship to be so built in England, she had to be replanked carvel-fashion in 1523 and was rebuilt as an ordinary sailing man-of-war in 1536–7 under the name *Great Bark*.[1]

What little we know about her as originally built is contained in letters written by the French and Venetian envoys in England. The first tells us that she had 120 oars and 207 guns, more even than the *Henry Grace a Dieu*; the second, which calls her 'a large galeass,' adds the information that her heavy guns were carried on a deck above the rowers, two forward and five aft on either side. Another scrap of knowledge is that she had, at least on one occasion, 160 rowers.

This must be considered in conjunction with her being called by the Venetians a galeass without further comment as to the disposition of her oars, for at this date Venetian galleys, both *sottili* and *grosse*, carried their oars in groups of three at one level with a single man on each; while the only simple way of employing 160 men on 120 oars would be to have 80 oars with one man each and 40 with two; in other words 40 groups of three with two men on the longest oar of a group and one on each of the others.

Considerations of space make something of the sort inevitable, for if 60 oars on each side were disposed in a single rank at intervals of 3 ft – the minimum possible – the length occupied by the rowers would be 180 ft and the ship impossibly long; whereas with the trireme grouping the distance between groups could be increased to as much as 5 ft – far more than would actually be required – and still let the ship's length be kept within reasonable limits.

Two smaller ships built in 1497 present the same problem of how their oars were arranged. The *Sweepstake* and *Mary Fortune* were of only 80 tons and yet carried 60 and 80 oars respectively; at the very most their keel-length may have been 60 ft and yet room was found for 30 or 40 oars a side. Probably they were biremes in the Venetian sense of the word, with oars in pairs where the *Great*

---

[1] For a fuller account of this ship's history see *The Mariner's Mirror*, 1920, pp. 274–281. The estimate there given of her dimensions should be ignored.

Galley had them in threes. If so, they repeated the probable arrangement of the English galleys of 200 years earlier.

It is hard to make any close estimate of the *Great Galley's* dimensions, because all we know is that she was rated at 800 tons without knowing whether that figure referred to what the Elizabethans called 'burthen' or to 'tons and tonnage,' the second being either $\frac{5}{4}$ or $\frac{4}{3}$ of the first. Perhaps a keel-length of 120–125 ft, a beam of 33–36 ft and a depth in hold of 16–17 ft will not be far wrong. These proportions are roughly those of the galeass *Bull* which will be mentioned shortly.

There is, however, a possibility that the remains of a ship discovered at Woolwich in 1912 were those of the *Great Galley* and in that case she was much wider than just suggested, at least in her rebuilt state. In his recent very thorough study of plans and photographs of these remains[1] Mr W. Salisbury came to the conclusion that the ship must have measured about 115–120 ft on the keel with a beam of at least 45 ft, proportions more suitable to a pure sailing ship than to one intended to work under oars at times. Fortunately the *Great Galley* is not the only possibility; the *Henry Grace a Dieu* cannot be dismissed altogether and the *Soverign* of 1509 has a still better cl im for consideration.

According to the Venetian account the *Great Galley* had four masts, of which three carried tops and topmasts, while the main topmast had a top of its own with a mast above it, so that she could set eight sails. This would be the normal rig of a large ship in the 16th century, with two mizzens, one carrying a topsail, but such a rig actually totalled nine sails with the spritsail. Apparently the writer forgot this sail; in those days there would be no sign of it unless it was actually in use.

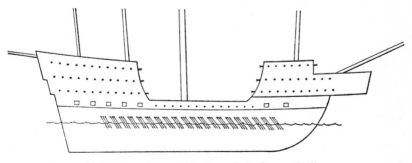

FIG. 15. *Conjectural broadside view of the* Great Galley, *1515*

[1] *The Mariner's Mirror*, 1961, pp. 81–90. See also *ibid.*, 1959, p. 98, for Laughton's two estimates.

There is one hint as to the ship's general design in the statement that the deck above the rowers was 'like a great plain.' This suggests that there was no deck above it and that the waist was longer than in the ordinary great ship of the time. There must, however, have been extensive superstructures forward and aft to accommodate the enormous number of small guns. The upper deck is also described as *ingaridata*. It is suggested in *State Papers, Venetian* that this means 'strewed with gravel,' but actually it means 'covered by an awning' like the poop of a galley. Probably the covering in this case consisted of gratings or perhaps only netting.

Some such ship as this must have been in the mind of the author of the sea scene in *The Complaynt of Scotland*, a work printed in 1549. In this he describes how 'ane galiasse gayly grathit for the veyr' gets under way to chase and engage an enemy. She was clearly a square-rigged ship with at least three masts and is said to have used 'ane hundreth aris on every side;' this can hardly mean 100 oars on each side, but may well mean 100 in all. It is certain that there was no such ship in Scotland at this time, for though the English navy contained two so-called galeasses taken from the Scots in 1544, these both belonged to what has been described above as the 'ill-defined class of ships without oars,' while their armament can never have been so large and so diversified as that catalogued by the Scottish writer. If he was trying to portray an actual ship, the *Great Galley* is the only possibility.

When we come to the English galeasses of 1546 we are on much firmer ground. We know more or less what they looked like afloat from Anthony Anthony's drawings, we have their midship section recorded in Baker's *Fragments of Ancient Shipwrightry*, as Pepys called it, and we probably know the dimensions of one of them, the *Bull*. That ship was rebuilt in 1570 and then lasted long enough to be included in a detailed list of 1591, the earliest list with dimensions that has yet been found. In it the *Bull*, originally rated at 200 tons, has a keel-length of 80 ft, a beam of 22 ft and a depth in hold of 11 ft, her 'burthen' being 193 tons. The ratio of keel to beam is almost $3\frac{2}{3}$, whereas the usual figure for contemporary ships of her size was about $2\frac{1}{2}$; this points very strongly to her having retained her original dimensions as an oared ship.

The drawing (Plate 10A) shows the *Bull* with 22 oar-ports on the broadside, all at one level and evenly spaced. A sheer-plan (Fig. 16) based on this and the dimensions just given, with the known rakes of stem and sternpost taken from the same list, puts that spacing at the very reasonable figure of approximately 3 ft 9 in. Judging by the number of the crew, 100 apart from 20 gunners, the oars may have been manned on occasion by two men each. There were six heavy guns on each broadside with two right forward and two in the stern, all apparently carried on a continuous deck above the rowers.

In the other 200-ton ship, the *Tiger*, there were 18 guns on this deck including the pair right forward, but the two stern guns and a pair near the after end of the projecting forecastle are shown at a higher level. It seems that there was a third deck running from end to end above the broadside guns; the increased freeboard amidships makes this almost certain. As for the *Hart* and *Antelope* of 300 tons, they are shown as almost exactly like the *Tiger* except for having one more gun on each side.

Pinnaces, built for the most part a year or two earlier, were small editions of the *Bull* and were about the same size as the *Mary Fortune* and *Sweepstake*, but had fewer oars, usually 20 a side, and

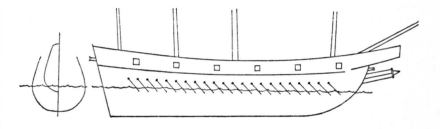

Fig. 16. *Conjectural broadside view of the* Bull, *1546*

carried these all at one level and evenly spaced. Row-barges were much smaller; they were of only 20 tons and rowed 15 oars a side with the usual pair of bow-chasers and a pair of guns on either side well aft. According to French accounts they were very long for their beam, even more so than ordinary galleys; they were probably about 50 ft on the keel and at the most 10 ft wide.

In rig the three classes showed a progressive simplification, but all three were definitely square-rigged. The galeasses were four-masted with fore and main topmasts; pinnaces had three masts with a topmast on the main only; row-barges had only the three courses without topsails. All had bowsprits and could presumably set spritsails.

Anthony Anthony's second 'roll,' from which the drawing of the *Bull* has been reproduced, includes among the galeasses a single oared vessel of quite different type, the *Galley Subtylle* of 1544 (Plate 10B). As her name suggests, she appears almost exactly like the ordinary Mediterranean fighting galley of her time, the *galia sottil*, but with one important difference, her oars are not grouped in threes as one would expect, but are evenly spaced. How many oars a side are shown is hard to say, but it is quite clear that the artist had no idea of showing them otherwise than running in a single line at regular intervals.

The matter of the change from oars *alla sensile* in groups of three each worked by one man to the system *al scaloccio* with oars evenly spaced and several men on each will be discussed in the next chapter. The new system was only on trial at Venice in 1534 and a writer in 1550 still gave measurements appropriate to the older arrangement, at least for the merchant-galleys which were about to develop into fighting galeasses. It is possible that the change had been made sooner at Genoa or elsewhere in the Mediterranean, but one can say at least that Henry VIII's one true galley was thoroughly up to date in the arrangement of her oars.

VIII

Southern Galleys Al Scaloccio

Fausto's quinquereme, launched at Venice in 1529, with her five men to a bank, each with his own oar, was the climax of the system of rowing *alla sensile* described in Chapter 6. Quadriremes with four oars to a bank had been built now and then for a century or more and it has been shown that a Genoese galley of 1535, also classed as a quadrireme, was probably rowed by oars in pairs with two men on each. There was a proposal at Venice as late as 1553 to repeat this arrangement, but that was the last attempt to retain anything like the old system; by then the new plan in which several men worked on one large oar had become almost universal.[1]

The first Venetian record of oars *di scaloccio*, as they were called, dates from 1534, when long oars for three men each were ordered to be sent to the fleet for trial. Quite possibly such oars were already in use elsewhere, but this cannot be proved at present. In 1551 the new system was applied to the merchant galleys which soon developed into the galeasses of Lepanto and by then it was probably well established in their lighter sisters. Experience soon showed that a three-man oar was less efficient than three oars each worked by one man, but four or five men to an oar proved a success and this became the general rule, though large galleys used as flagships might have six or even seven men to an oar.[2]

Some dimensions of galleys of various dates and nationalities may be compared with those given in Chapter 6; they have been converted to English measure to the nearest $\frac{1}{4}$ ft. In most cases there are two sets of figures, for standard galleys and for flagships.[3]

---

[1] Fincati, *Le Trireme* (1881), p. 7. Lane, *Venetian Ships and Shipbuilders* (1934), p. 31.

[2] Pantero Pantera, *L'Armata Navale* (1614), p. 150.

[3] The sources are as follows:— 1, MS. *Visione di Drachio* quoted by Lane, *Venetian Ships and Shipbuilders*, p. 242. 2, Crescentio, *Nautica Mediterranea*, pp. 11-13, 25. 3, De Barros, *As Galés Portuguesas* (1930). 4, Furttenbach, *Architectura Navalis*. 5, Katip Celebi

		Length	Beam	Banks	Length	Beam	Banks
1	Venetian 1593 ...	142½	17 (25)	—	—	—	—
2	Neapolitan 1607 ...	143	18 (24)	—	—	—	—
3	Portuguese 1616 ...	145	17¼	24	152	19¾ (25¼)	28
4	Maltese 1629 ...	143½	20	—	151½	20	27
5	Turkish c. 1655 ...	135	—	25	160½	—	36
6	French c. 1670 ...	140½	19	25	—	—	—
7	Venetian 1686 ...	142	18 (24)	—	167¼	22¼	—
8	Venetian c. 1690 ...	135½	17	—	170	22½	—
9	French 1691	153½	19 (25¾)	—	—	—	—
10	French c. 1725 ...	152	19¼	26	168½	21¼	29
11	Tuscan c. 1725 ...	155	20¼	26	166½	21¼	29
12	Venetian c. 1725 ...	146	18½	25	165½	20¾	28
13	Maltese c. 1725 ...	155	20¾	26	169½	21½	29
14	French (?) 1745 ...	—	—	—	163	21¼ (32½)	30
15	Maltese c. 1750 ...	—	—	—	179½	24¼ (34)	30
16	Maltese c. 1770 ...	—	—	—	160	(32½)	29

The change from the one system of rowing to the other caused very little change in the general design of galleys, since all that was needed was to fit a single thole-pin in place of a group and provide heavier oars to be worked by several men each. An old-fashioned trireme was probably too narrow to accommodate side by side the four men found to be the minimum required for efficiency, but there is no difficulty in believing that Fausto's quinquereme or even a quadrireme could be converted to the new method of rowing with very little modification.

A Venetian trireme's longest oars had measured about 32 ft. Furttenbach (1629) gives a scale-drawing of a five-man oar 38½ ft long and Fournier (1643) mentions oars of 43 ft. At the beginning of the 18th century the smaller galleys used oars of about 38 ft and the flagships 41 ft or more.

Furttenbach's drawing shows that four men of the crew of five used hand-grips fitted on the fore side of the oar, while the fifth

---

(see note on p. 78). 6, Dassié, *L'Architecture Navale* (1677). 7, Sttefano de Zuanne, MS. British Museum Add.38655. 8, Coronelli, *Atlante Veneto* (section 'de Navigli') p. 140. 9, Establishment printed by Saverien, *Dictionnaire de Marine* (1758) s.v. Galere. 10–13, Falkengren MS. (see *The Mariner's Mirror*, 1956, p. 181). 14, Draught No. 6441/58, National Maritime Museum. 15, Chapman, *Architectura Navalis Mercatoria*, Plate 58. 16, Model No. 1770–3, National Maritime Museum.

The scales of Nos. 14 and 16 are not quite certain. The number of banks in the larger Turkish galley may be a mistake, though Fournier (1643) writing at almost the same date mentions that the Turkish flag-galley had 33 banks as against 28 or 29 for those of France and Spain. Chapman's 'La Capitana' (No. 15) must have been exceptionally large, but his authority leaves little doubt that the figures are correct.

worked on a thinner prolongation of the loom similar to that on any sea-boat's oar today, but longer. It also shows that each man was allowed just less than 2 ft of space and that the outermost sat about 4 ft from the thole-pin. These figures are worth mentioning as a guide to what was practicable in the days of the polyremes.

The term *remo di scaloccio* is not easy to explain. Authorities agree that the word scaloccio is related to *scala*, a ladder or staircase, but cannot say why this should be the case. Perhaps the ladder was formed by the cross-pieces connecting the long set of hand-grips to the oar between each pair of men; the appearance of the whole arrangement is not unlike that of a very narrow ladder with one upright very much thicker than the other. This is no more than a suggestion, but I hope not too far-fetched.

The innermost man on an oar was called the *vogavante* or in French *vogue avant*. At first sight one would take this to mean that he faced forward and pushed instead of pulling, but this was not so; he was simply the foreman of the gang and responsible for his crew's keeping time. This is another term which needs explaining. It cannot have been taken over from the old system, because there the innermost man of a group of three was not the foremost, but slightly the aftermost.

Since the Mediterranean galley was almost a standardised product with the pattern remaining practically unchanged for 200 years or more, it is natural that its armament should have varied very little. There was always one heavy gun, the *cannone di corsia* or in French the *coursier*, carried on the centre line at the fore end of the *corsia* or fore-and-aft gangway and firing over the beak and close above it; there were lighter guns on each side of this also firing forward and there were secondary light pieces on the broadside and aft for defence rather than attack.

Guglielmotti prints a list of the guns needed for a Florentine galley in 1574.[1] They were: one 50-pr *cannone*, two 10-pr *sagri* (sakers), two 4-pr *mezzi sagri* (or two 12-pr *petriere*) and finally eight 4-pr breech-loading *smerigli*. No doubt the first five pieces were mounted forward and the rest on the sides.

Pantero Pantera (1614) makes the sakers 8- or 9-prs and the *petrieros* 15-prs and adds a *smeriglio* on either side forward and another pair of two small *petrieros* aft. He mentions that the Venetians carried also a number of *falconetti a cavallo* (on swivels) above the *coursier* and its supporters. Furttenbach (1629) gives a *halb carthaun* (probably a 32-pr) flanked by a pair of 10-pr *moiane*

---

[1] *Storia della Marina Pontificia*, Vol. 4, p. 166.

or sakers with a pair of 9-pr breech-loading *petrieros* outside them. He describes the galleys of Naples, Florence and Malta as carrying also a 2-pr falconet and a ½-pr *smeriglio* on either side at the fore end of the *telaro*, so that there were actually 9 pieces in a line athwartships all firing forward.[1]

He tells us also that only the single big gun was on a recoiling carriage, the others were on fixed mountings. A print after Bruegel shows galleys of about 1550 with their guns, apart from the *coursier*, mounted on top of heavy uprights like exaggerated swivel-stocks, but Furttenbach's own illustrations suggest that by his time these mountings were well on the way towards becoming normal carriages. How soon this took place and how soon all the guns firing forward were allowed to recoil as the *coursier* did is uncertain. In French galleys the two 12-pr *bâtardes* next to the *coursier* were on recoiling mountings before 1677[2] and by the end of the century all five guns firing forward were on similar truckless carriages sliding in fore-and-aft troughs.[3] So they remained to the end.

In 1614 Pantero Pantera noted the Venetian practice of carrying guns above the *coursier* as well as beside it. This was still usual towards the end of the century, for a manuscript of 1686 gives a typical armament as a 20-pr *coursier* with two 12-pr *falconets* above it and three 12-pr *petrieros* on either side; there were two more of these on each broadside and two aft. Coronelli's *Atlante Veneto* of almost the same date makes the *coursier* a 50-pr, but this was for a flagship as opposed to an ordinary private galley.

The well known compilation *L'Art de Bâtir les Vaisseaux*, printed in Holland in 1719, copies the dimensions given by Furttenbach 90 years earlier and some of his plates, but comments that 'nowadays' in French galleys the 34-pr *coursier* is flanked by two 26-prs instead of by four smaller guns. This may have been true when the words were written, but we know that in 1697 and again in 1725 the majority of galleys, French or foreign, had five guns forward, a *coursier* firing a shot of between 24 and 42 lbs (English) and four smaller guns, about 8-prs; while on the broadside they might have as many as 20 small swivel-guns.[4]

Finally we have the armament given by Chapman for his Maltese *Capitana*: one 36-pr, two 9-pr, two 6-pr, 18 swivels and 18 musket-

---

[1] No attempt has been made to allow for differences in the various 'pounds.'

[2] Dassié, *Architecture Navale*, p. 141.

[3] MS. of 1697 by Barras de la Penne on the construction of galleys, reproduced in part by Paris in *Souvenirs de Marnie*, Vol. 5. There is a very closely related MS. in the National Maritime Museum.

[4] See *The Mariner's Mirror*, 1956, p. 182.

PLATE 14A. Neapolitan galeass off Terceira, 1583. Fresco in the Escorial, Madrid

PLATE 14B. Neapolitan galeass in the Armada, 1588. National Maritime Museum

PLATE 15. Venetian galeasses in the Dardanelles, 1655. Contemporary
drawing. National Gallery of Scotland

PLATE 16A. Venetian galeass, *c.* 1710. Model in Danish Admiralty collection

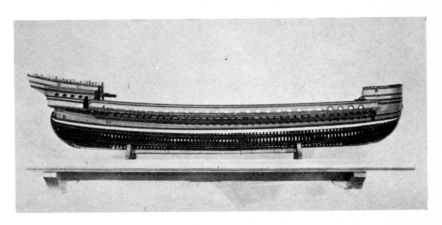

PLATE 16B. Venetian galeass, *c.* 1670. Model in Central Naval Museum, Leningrad

PLATE 17A. Venetian galeass, *c.* 1690. From *Neptune Francois*

PLATE 17B. Florentine 'bastardella' (?), *c.* 1640. Drawing by Baccio del
Bianco. Uffizi Gallery, Florence

oons. It is a pity that no exact date can be ascribed to this vessel. She must have been built before 1768, when his book was printed, and it is probable that he used draughts as far as possible up to date. Perhaps 1750 is a fair estimate.

The first galleys *al scaloccio* were rigged, as their predecessors *alla sensile* had been, with one mast and one large lateen sail. This was still the rig of the galleys at Lepanto in 1571, but by 1600 at latest a two-masted rig was universal. The temporary foremast with a small square sail, mentioned in Chapter 6, as seen occasionally in the 15th century had become a permanent fitting and now carried a lateen with a yard about half as long as that of the mainsail. This foremast was placed just abaft the yoke at the fore end of the rowing space and raked forward over the prow and beak; it had to be stepped on one side or other of the trough in which the big gun recoiled. Sometimes, at a later date, it was stepped on the forecastle deck above the gun, but the off-centre arrangement was by far the more usual. The mainmast had moved aft a little, though hardly as much as one would expect; its new position was still well before the midship section and there it remained as long as galleys were built.

The foresail of a sailing ship began as no more than a balancing sail and grew bit by bit until it was not far short of the mainsail in area. In galleys the process went even farther, for in the early part of the 18th century the fore yard was sometimes just longer than the main. Taking the length of the main yard as 100 in each case we find that Furttenbach (1629) makes the fore yard about 60, while Dassié (1677) makes it 90, Barras de la Penne (1697) 98 and Falkengren (1725) about 101 for French practice. According to the same authority the Venetians also had fore yards just longer than the main in 1725, but the Maltese and Tuscans had not yet gone so far and perhaps never did.

Occasionally there was also a small mizzen set on a mast just before the poop. It is found more often in models than in prints or drawings and in every case where it appears the date seems to be well on in the 18th century, but it must be mentioned that Crescentio lists a mizzen as far back as 1607, when even the second mast must have been a comparative novelty. Coronelli (1692) says that 'sometimes to make more speed, they add a little mizzen (*mezzan-ello*)' and that is probably the explanation. Model-makers in particular have always tended to give their ships any item of gear of which they had knowledge; some of the French prisoner models show this very well.

The last occasion when Mediterranean galleys took part in any

large scale fighting was at the battle of Matapan in 1717, where
the Christian fleet contained galleys provided by Venice, the Pope,
the Knights of Malta and the Grand Duke of Tuscany. They do not
seem to have had much influence on the outcome of the battle,
such as it was, and next year they were not allowed to come in
contact with the enemy. After that the Mediterranean, or rather
its eastern basin, enjoyed a long period of peace, broken only by
the Russian incursion in 1770, and galley warfare became a thing
of the past. Nothing more is heard of Tuscan galleys after 1718;
at Naples in 1734 there were only four galleys and these very old;
the French galley service was abolished in 1748. Only Venice, the
Pope and the Knights of Malta continued to use galleys until the
seizure of their fleets by Bonaparte. When the French entered
Venice in 1797 there were actually three galleys under construction
besides 20 others either there or at Corfu; while the Papal flotilla
still contained three efficient galleys and at Malta there were four
in commission to the last, one of them built as recently as 1796.
Their new owners made no use of them. The day of the galley
al scaloccio and its five-man oars was at an end.

Even so, the story of oared men-of-war in the Mediterranean was
not quite finished; it was continued for a few years by the half-
galley, in particular by two vessels of this class built for the Papal
fleet in 1796. The term half-galley had long been in use for a small
edition of the galley *al scaloccio*, but these were different in one
important respect; they still had the *apostis* or outrigger, but they
had only one man to an oar and these were part of the ordinary
crew, not slaves or convicts.

They were about 100 ft long and 20 ft wide over all and they
had 20 oars on each side. Their armament consisted of one 24-pr,
two 12-prs and eight swivels, the larger guns firing forward in the
usual way.[1]

These two late descendants of the classical galley proved their
seaworthiness in the French expedition to Egypt in 1798 and did
good work in the fighting on the Nile, but after that they vanished.
By the time Alexandria was retaken by British and Turkish forces
in 1801 they had probably been broken up for firewood. It may be
that the five French half-galleys captured by the Russians and Turks
at Corfu in 1799 had been built in imitation of these Papal ships,
but nothing is known about them beyond the fact that they were
given to the new Ionian Republic in 1800. If they remained afloat,
they probably passed into French hands in 1807 and back to their

---

[1] Guglielmotti, Vol. 9, p. 290.

former owners in 1814, the year in which a final pair of half-galleys was launched for the Sardinian navy. These two vessels, rowing 17 oars a side and so probably a little smaller than their Papal predecessors, were the last representatives of a family which can be traced back for at least 2,500 years.

IX

The Galeass

In the 15th century Venetian galleys were of two very distinct kinds, the *galia sottil* for fighting and the *galia grosa* as a long-voyage merchantman;[1] the two names correspond to 'light' and 'heavy.' The larger type was also called a *galeassa* and it was under that name or some variation of it that the fighting ship developed from it was always known.

As a merchantman the galeass had carried only light guns for self-defence; the addition of heavy guns firing forward made it into a formidable man-of-war. The change began in the middle of the 16th century and the new type proved its worth at Lepanto in 1571 with the result that galeasses formed an important part of the Venetian fleet for nearly 150 years. They were, indeed, described towards the end of the 17th century as its chief strength, though by then, with the sailing battleship becoming supreme even in the Mediterranean, their day was nearly over. They saw their last active service in 1715 in spite of the fact that the war then beginning had another three years to run.

The *mahona* used by the Turks in the Cretan war of 1645–1669 was very similar and had also been derived from an oared merchant-man or transport, while ships of the same type were built by Naples, Florence and perhaps France; but it was only in the Venetian navy that the galeass played an important part for any great length of time.

The standard Venetian merchant-galley of the middle of the 16th century was about 157 ft long and 26 ft wide on the true hull or 33 ft over the *apostis* on either side.[2] The length had remained

---

[1] Spellings differed widely. The forms given here are those used by Timbotta, a Venetian, in 1445.

[2] All measurements have been converted to English feet (approximately). The Venetian foot was roughly equal to 13½ in. English.

almost constant for 100 years, but the beam had grown by 6 ft or more. These were probably the dimensions of the galeasses used at Lepanto, whether newly built or, as seems more likely, converted from trading vessels. They were rowed on the newly introduced system *al scaloccio* with large oars each worked by three or four men in contrast to the old *alla sensile* fashion in which the oars were disposed in groups of three with a single man on each.

This matter of how the oars were arranged has to be considered in some detail because of a slight conflict of evidence. Casoni relied on a single print, admittedly contemporary, for his insistence that the galeasses of Lepanto carried their oars in groups of three as their mercantile predecessors had done.[1] Jal described this as *une grave erreur* and pointed out that no other representation or description of these vessels even hinted at such an arrangement.[2] There can be little doubt that Jal was right; the only other evidence for grouped oars at this date seems to be on the marble altar of a Venetian church, where both galleys and galeasses are shown with oars in *pairs*, an arrangement which must have been superseded, except in small craft, nearly 200 years before Lepanto.[3] In any case, we now know that the new system had been introduced in merchant-galeasses in 1551[4] and this amply confirms Jal's verdict. Artists who show grouped oars must have been either ignorant of recent developments or deliberately old-fashioned.[5]

As might have been expected, these first fighting galeasses proved slow and unwieldy in comparison with galleys of the same number of oars. Increasing the number of banks would have involved lengthening the hull and so making it heavier and more difficult to turn; the obvious alternative was to lengthen the oars and put more men to work on each. This, of course, meant increasing the width between thole-pins, but that could be done by a simple widening of the *telaro* or 'rowing frame' without adding to the width of the true hull. Each oar was then worked by five men.[6]

Ships of every class have always tended to become larger as time went on, but this tendency was less marked in those using oars, except in the days of the great Hellenistic polyremes. Fifty years after Lepanto, Venetian galeasses were barely 10 per cent longer and wider than when they first became fighting ships and after

[1] *Dei Navigli Poliremi — — Veneziani*, 1838, p. 45.

[2] *Archéologie Navale*, 1840, Vol. 1, p. 395.

[3] Nebbia, *Arte Naval Italiana*, 1932, p. 87.

[4] Lane, *Venetian Ships and Shipbuilders*, 1934, p. 31 n.

[5] My own 'attempt to combine several portraits' of the Lepanto galeasses (*The Sailing Ship*, 1926, p. 133) should have about 25 single oars substituted for the 11 groups of three.

[6] Lane, p. 33.

that there was no further increase. Furttenbach (1629) gives their dimensions as 172 ft by 28½ ft full, with 28 oars a side and six men on each,[1] and Fournier (1643) agrees that this length was the best.[2] Later on a Venetian shipbuilder writing in 1686 makes their length 165 ft or sometimes 170½ ft and their beam 28¼ ft bare, while his deck-plan shows that the width over all was then 35¼ ft.[3] (See Plate 13B.)

Two other sources of dimensions are less satisfactory. Coronelli, writing within a few years of 1690, agrees in giving a length of 165 ft but makes the width of the true hull only 24 ft and that over all 42 ft, figures very far from probable, if not actually impossible.[4] His illustration is also by no means convincing, but he does give useful information about the armament and the oars, 25 on one side and 24 on the other, each 47¾ ft long and worked by seven men.[5]

Crescentio, whose book was printed in 1607, deals very thoroughly with the design of galleys, but tells us less about galeasses, and though he states that his measurements are in Neapolitan *cubiti e palmi* and that there were three palms to a cubit, he leaves it for us to discover their relation to any other measure; the only clue is that seven palms is described as 'the height of a man.'[6]

If we take this as 6 ft English, we get a value for the *palmo* of 261 mm.; this is much greater than Furttenbach's figure and is in fact precisely that recorded for the *palmo* once used at Nice. This may be only a coincidence, but the Neapolitan *palmo* established by law in 1840 and probably very close to that already in use was only 3 mm. greater.[7] Using this value we get 6.1 ft for the headroom in the forecastle and 25.8 ft for the beam, both very reasonable figures; but when we come to length we find ourselves in difficulties, because Crescentio gives rakes forward and aft of 22 *palmi* each and a keel of 62 *cubiti* (186 *palmi*). The total of 230 *palmi* or 197½ ft is impossibly large and we can only suppose that what he calls the length on the keel was really that from stem to sternpost – including

---

[1] *Architectura Navalis*, p. 79. Although writing in German he gives measurements in *palmi*, explaining on p. 19 that these are equal to 10 in. of Nuremberg measure. The Bavarian foot was equal to 292 mm. and Furttenbach's *palmo* therefore 243 mm. or just over 9½ in. English. To make the matter even more certain he actually shows the length of a *palmo* on his Plate 2 and this, in the copy measured, is 242 mm.

[2] *Hydrographie*, p. 49. I have assumed that his *paume* was 9 in. French, again 243 mm.

[3] 'L'Architettura Navale di Sttefano de Zuanne de Michel — — in Venezia L'Anno 1686.' British Museum, Add. MSS. 38655. See Plates 13A and B.

[4] *Atlante Veneto* (section *De Navigli*), p. 141.

[5] The place of the missing oar was occupied by the cook-room. The illustration shows only 23 oars.

[6] *Nautica Mediterranea*, pp. 13, 58–61, 110.

[7] Figures for obsolete measures are from a Danish book, Bauer's *Haandbog i Mont-, Maal- og Vaegtforhold*, 1882, an extremely thorough work on the subject.

the rakes, not additional to them. This would give a length of 159¾ ft and make the dimensions very close to those recorded for the galeasses of 1571.[1]

A very fine model of a galeass in the Danish Admiralty collection (Plate 16A) is known to have been brought home in about 1740 by an officer sent to study the rowing men-of-war of the Mediterranean. It is almost certainly Venetian in origin, but it is hard to say whether it represents one of the last galeasses built there at the beginning of the century or its maker's idea of what a new vessel of the type should be. On the whole I am inclined to look on it as a model of an actual ship and to put its date about 1710, but I may well be wrong in both conclusions.

Its scale appears to be ¾ in. Venetian to 1 ft of 16 in. or $\frac{1}{21\cdot3}$; this makes the length from stem to sternpost 169 ft and the distance between oars about 4 ft 2 in., figures which agree well with those of the 1686 manuscript; on the other hand the projection of the outrigger is a good deal greater, the hull-beam working out at 27¼ ft and that over all at 40½ ft. The stern is without the long overhanging poop of the earlier galeasses and has a sternpost not far from straight, though not quite so emphatically so as that shown in the 'reformed' stern of 1686.

As a contrast a model of roughly the same size in the Central Naval Museum of Leningrad (Plate 16B), described as a Venetian galley of about 1700, but plainly a galeass and probably not later than 1670, has a sternpost forming almost a quadrant of a circle. The model is damaged or incomplete, but what it shows is almost exactly like the 1686 design in its unreformed state.

Now comes what ought to be the most reliable evidence of all, the very large model in the Museo Storico Navale of Venice. Unfortunately there are several very doubtful points about this model. Jal tells us that it was just being completed when he was in Venice in 1834[2] and we do not know what plans its builder was using. Its head suggests that of a sailing ship of the latter part of the 18th century and the brick-like sides forward can only be explained as a misunderstanding of some such drawing as that of 1686; the bowsprit too is a very suspicious feature. If galeasses had still been being built about 1780, they might have been like the

---

[1] Jal, *Archéologie Navale*, Vol. 1, p. 284, took the Neapolitan *palmo* as equivalent to the *pan* of Marseilles because he found the same figure, 58 cubits, given by contemporary writers for the length of standard galleys in the two ports. He went on to fix the value of the *pan* as 9 in. French or 243 mm., whereas it should be 251 mm. Such a value would make Crescentio's galeass distinctly too small.

[2] *Glossaire Nautique*, p. 739, with a good broadside drawing. Jal's measurements differ slightly from those given me by the Museum.

model, but that is the best one can say for it. The scale appears to be $\frac{1}{10}$ – a decimal scale would be natural at the time the model was made – and the dimensions of the actual ship would be roughly 167 ft stem to sternpost and 30¼ ft beam or 39 ft over all.

It is quite likely that the galeass which Crescentio described in his book of 1607 was not Venetian but Neapolitan. His illustration, apparently drawn from a rather rough model, shows a ship almost exactly like one in a picture painted in 1590 of the Spanish fleet off Terceira in 1583 (Plate 14A).[1] That fleet included two galeasses and there were four, from Naples, in the Armada of 1588, at least one of them returning to Spain in safety. Unfortunately there are no good portraits of these Armada galeasses, for engravings from lost tapestries based on unknown designs can hardly be taken as evidence. Such as they are, the prints show the galeasses with square rig and the natural tendency is to look on this as a mistake, but that may not be the case. Crescentio tells us that 'in Spain they have given them square rig' and it may well be that they had been rerigged for the voyage to England and that the tapestries and a supposedly contemporary painting in the National Maritime Museum (Plate 14B) were right in showing them thus. As far as we know, in her home in the Mediterranean the galeass kept her three-masted lateen rig to the last.

The Turks used ships of this kind only for a few years during the Cretan war of 1645–1669; the *maone* included in the fleet sent against Malta in 1565 were almost certainly mere oared transports similar to the Venetian merchant-galleys. Coronelli tells us that *maone* were bigger than galeasses, but less effective in action. They may have been wider and heavier, but their length, as recorded by a contemporary Turkish writer,[2] was slightly less than that of a Venetian galeass, 160 ft. As drawn by Italian observers they were very like their opponents except for a slight difference in the shape of the stern.[3]

There remain the galeasses of Florence or Tuscany and possibly of France. All that can be said of the former is that 'the two

---

[1] Reproduced in *The Mariner's Mirror*, 1949, p. 115, from Tenison's *Elizabethan England*. The painting shows only 21 oars a side, whereas Crescentio's drawing has 30 and the other picture 32.

[2] Katip Celebi (or Haji Khalifeh), who died in 1657. The first part of his *Maritime Wars of the Turks* was published in translation in 1831. He gives details of several oared craft with the *mavna* of 26 banks (7 men to an oar) and 24 guns as the largest. Notes supplied to me through Col H. I. Chapelle give dimensions in metres.

[3] See *The Mariner's Mirror*, 1919, p. 59. The statement by Pantero Pantera, *L'Armata Navale*, p. 42, that *maone* were like Venetian galeasses, 'but do not go with oars' is more than doubtful even for his time and certainly untrue of the fighting *maone* of 40 years later. Perhaps the word 'well' was omitted in printing.

galeasses of the Duke of Florence' were included in the order of battle of the Christian fleet of 1572;[1] after that nothing is heard of them beyond the fact that they were still in existence in 1588, but considered failures.[2]

The drawings of Baccio del Bianco (1604–1656) include among many very good sketches of Florentine galleys a few examples of oared vessels of a heavier type with guns on the broadside well above the oars and the rig of a *caravela redonda*, a square-rigged foremast with three lateens abaft it.[3] (Plate 17B.) If there had been galeasses in the Tuscan fleet in, say, 1625–1650, we might suppose that in spite of the obvious differences between them and their Venetian contemporaries these were also galeasses. As it is, we have to find another name for them and it seems possible that they may be *bastardelle*, of which three were built in 1601–5 and one was still afloat in 1646. Bastarda was, as has been seen, a common name for an extra-large galley, though usually implying little difference in general design from her smaller sisters. The identification is far from satisfactory, but it is hard to suggest an alternative.

The finest and best known model of a galeass is that of *La Royale* in the French Musée de Marine. There are plans, photographs and a detailed description of this model in Vol. 2 of *Souvenirs de Marine*, the great work of Admiral Pâris, but unfortunately it is very far from certain that there ever was a galeass of that name in the French navy, or indeed that galeasses were ever built in France. They never appear in lists of fleets and it would be very strange for this to be so if they really existed. Pâris refers to a French manuscript of 1690 and to two drawings by Jouve dated 1679, but one of these reproduced by La Roërie and Vivielle in *Navires et Marins* shows a Venetian ensign quite clearly.[4] As for *La Royale*, it has been shown that a very large proportion of French models were made 'pour eux-mêmes' without representing actual ships. What is more, the model, when first brought to Paris, contained a label with the word 'Projet'. Admiral Pâris took this to apply only to the spars for an alternative square rig, but it may just as well have referred to the model as a whole.

Still, this is so important a model that it seems desirable to make

---

[1] Printed by Aparigi, *Coleccion de Documentos* — — — *Lepanto*, 1847, and wrongly ascribed to 1571.

[2] Manfroni, *La Marina da Guerra di Cosimo I.* — —, in *Rivista Marittima*, 1895.

[3] One of these drawings in the Uffisi Gallery, Florence, was reproduced in *Dedalo*, 1932, p. 861. The National Maritime Museum has photographs of drawings in a private collection showing exactly similar vessels and apparently by the same hand.

[4] This drawing was cribbed by Gueroult du Pas in 1710 and called by him 'Galeasse de Venise.'

an effort to establish the true dimensions of the ship represented, even if she was never built, and here we run into difficulties at once. Pâris put two scales on his plans, one trying to bring the model into agreement with the figures in the manuscript of 1690, the other based on an assumed value of 1.40 metres (4.6 ft) for the distance between thole-pins. These scales are indicated as 0.057 and 0.049; expressed in another way they are $\frac{1}{17.5}$ and $\frac{1}{20.4}$.

Now a French model maker in those days would not work on any sort of decimal scale but on some fraction of an inch to a foot[1] and that fraction would almost certainly be capable of being expressed in lines or twelfths of an inch. If he wanted a larger fraction than $\frac{1}{2}$, his choice would probably be $\frac{2}{3}$, *i.e.* eight lines to 1 ft (or 1 in. to $1\frac{1}{2}$ ft). To take even $\frac{7}{12}$, which works out at $\frac{1}{20.57}$ and is not far from the suggested $\frac{1}{20.4}$, would be most unlikely.

Even with the scale thus fixed as $\frac{1}{18}$ some calculation is needed before the dimensions of this – perhaps imaginary – galeass can be compared with those of other ships of the class. The larger set of figures given by Pâris have to be multiplied by $\frac{18}{20.4}$ and then converted from metres to feet (English). In the end we get a length of 168 ft, a hull-beam of $33\frac{1}{2}$ ft and a width over all of $41\frac{1}{2}$ ft, while the distance between oars works out at just over 4 ft. Actually the plans show a larger interval than that postulated by Pâris and make the result $4\frac{1}{4}$ ft.[2]

The ship of the 1690 manuscript would have been 164 ft long and 32 ft wide or 37 ft over all; her outriggers would thus have been considerably narrower, but the interval between oars the same. She would have had 25 banks with nine men on some oars and eight on the rest. The model has only 21 banks, but the oars, if fully manned, would appear to have had 19 men on each.

This is little short of incredible. It is true that the oars found with the model do show nine hand-holds on each side and another on the end, but even Pâris had to admit that these oars were impossibly large and suggested making them 50 ft, as in the manuscript, instead of 71 ft. He realised that this would involve lowering the *apostis* or sinking the whole ship deeper, to let the oars reach the water, but failed to notice that this unjustified tampering with the scale would mean accommodating nine men in a width of little more than 10 ft.

---

[1] The fact that the French foot was larger than the English does not affect the reasoning at this stage.

[2] The catalogue of the Musée de Marine (1909) adopts the dimensions given by Saverien in 1758, 171 ft by 34 ft English. This requires an inexplicable scale of $\frac{1}{18.3}$ and produces an error of nearly 20 ft in the length of the keel. Saverien's figures were, admittedly, no more than a proposal.

Is there any evidence from the 17th century or the beginning of the 18th, apart from this one model and its very doubtful oars, for the manning of oars on both sides on a push-and-pull system? I know of none and should be surprised to learn that it exists.[1] Certainly I do not believe that such an arrangement was possible with oars little more than 4 ft apart in spite of Pâris's drawing showing how he thought it might have been managed. To tell the truth, Pâris is far from clear in this connection; it is hard to say whether he is trying to explain the 19 men of the model or the nine of the manuscript. The latter we must accept as at least a possibility, though other nations seem to have been content with seven men to an oar, but 19 is beyond belief. Perhaps the explanation of the two rows of hand-holds is that the oar was reversible; that would at least be a way of reducing the wear at the thole-pin.

A strange and even suspicious feature of this French model is the way in which the stern planking takes a very sudden reversed concave curve just short of the sternpost; stranger still is the fact that the plans do not show this, though it appears very clearly in one of the photographs. What the plans show is not far from the normal stern *alla bastarda* or *alla faustina* in which the sternpost curved through nearly two-thirds of a circle till it was actually raking forward at the top and the planking also curved through more than 90° and left the sternpost in a definite depression. The French name for this form of stern, *cul de monine* or monkey's bottom, is sufficiently descriptive.

The explanation of the two Italian names is that this form of stern, which gave extra width aft without altering the rake, was to be found in *bastarde* or extra-large galleys and had perhaps been introduced by the famous Vettor Fausto, mentioned in connection with the solitary quinquereme *alla sensile*. It was afterwards modified by lengthening the keel and straightening the lower part of the sternpost while still leaving the upper planking much as it was. According to Sttefano de Zuanne this improvement was first made by him in 1669 to facilitate the hanging of a normal stern-rudder *alla ponentina*, in Western fashion.

A galeass had a strongly built forecastle and carried her main armament forward, as a galley did. There were other fairly heavy guns aft and a number of light pieces on the broadside above or between the oars. We do not know the armament of the Venetian galeasses at Lepanto, but we have exact figures for the four Neapolitans in 1587. They carried 29 or 30 guns ranging from

---

[1] I must admit having accepted the possibility of such an arrangement in the great Hellenistic ships, but any alternative explanation of their design would be welcome.

50-pr to 6-pr and as many as 60 smaller pieces, some no more than
½-pr. At least four and probably six of the heavier guns could fire
forward.[1]

Crescentio tells us only that a galeass had two *corsie* or heavy guns
firing forward over the beak in place of the single gun in a galley,
but Pantero Pantera is far more informative. According to him
there were about 70 guns all told. The two *corsie* had another pair
of lighter guns outside them and there were perhaps 10 others in
or below the forecastle of sizes running from 30-pr to 5-pr. There
were also eight similar guns aft and a perrier, a short gun with a
heavy shot, between each pair of banks. He mentions an arrangement
by which the recoil of one *corsia* brought the other into the firing
position.

Furttenbach gives his galeass a total of only 35 guns. He puts
five big and four small forward and two right aft, as in a ship's
gunroom; the 12 guns on each side above the rowers are clearly
stated to be small swivel-pieces. It will be seen that he says nothing
of any guns aft apart from the two stern-chasers. Fournier mentions
only the guns above the rowers, 10 on each side.

The only list that can be considered official is that of Sttefano de
Zuanne (1686) and it is fortunate that he goes into details. In the
forecastle there were two 50-pr, outside these two long 14's, two
perriers of the same calibre and two 6-pr falcons. Firing aft there
were two 30's with two 14's outside them in the *corridori da pupa*
(corresponding roughly to quarter-galleries) and two 3-pr above.
On each broadside among the oars there were four 20-pr, one of
them firing forward from the end of the *apostis*, and four 14-pr
perriers. All save these last can be located in his plans.

Coronelli gives a different armament, two 50's, two 30's and six
6's forward with two 30's, four long 14's, 12 14-pr perriers and two
others of as much as 120 lb. somewhere aft and along the sides.
Another list in Aubin's *Dictionnaire de Marine* (1702) gives two 36's,
two 24's and two 10's forward and 12 18's aft, emphasising the fact
that the guns forward were on three levels and those aft on two.
When we consider that since the middle of the 17th century only
the Venetians had built galeasses and that in very small numbers,
it seems strange that there should be such diversity in the accounts
of their armament.

Although, as has been said, it is unlikely that there ever were
French galeasses, it is as well to end with the armaments allotted
to what must at least have been French projects. Pâris tells us that

---

[1] Duro, *La Armada Invencible*, Vol. 1, p. 389. It is quite likely that they carried more
guns in 1588. See Lewis, 'Armada Guns' in *The Mariner's Mirror*, 1943, p. 15 *et al.*

the manuscript of 1690 gives 30 cannon (using the term in a general sense), 18 perriers and 14 swivels. The model of *La Royale* has six big and six small guns forward, four firing aft on two levels and six under the quarter-deck; there are seven on either broadside *below* the oars and 22 swivels on the rails and the *apostis*.[1] Finally there is Saverien's proposed galeass of about 1750 with four 36's and two 12's firing forward, two 48's and two 12's firing aft, six 6's and two 4's on the broadside, 30 2-pr swivels and finally a 12-in. mortar on the forecastle. It is as well that we can be sure that his ship is merely a project, because he had begun his article by lifting Aubin's description and that included an entirely different armament.

It has been mentioned that the number of galeasses built was small. Even in Venice, where they were in use for nearly 150 years, the number in service at any one time was never more than seven and usually less. One Turkish fleet contained as many as 10, but that was only as a swan-song; elsewhere we can only find two Tuscans and four Neapolitans. This type of vessel had an important place in the story of rowing men-of-war, but only within narrow limits of both space and time.

---

[1] Pâris gives 34 guns in his text, but his plans show 36.

X

Hybrids of the 17th and 18th Centuries

We have seen that there was a galley of southern type in the English fleet in 1411 and another in 1545, but between these dates such vessels were probably unknown in England. Henry IV's *Jesu Maria* was soon no more than a source of spare parts[1] and in little more than 10 years the Royal Navy was rapidly ceasing to exist in any form. When the revival came under the first two Tudors, some oared vessels were indeed built, but these – even when called galleys – were quite unlike their namesakes in the Mediterranean. Henry VIII's rowbarges proved able to stand up to French galleys of much greater size and cost and he was content to build only the one *Galley Subtille* as an experiment, importing Italian shipwrights for the purpose.

This galley and another, the *Galley Blanchard* taken from the French in 1546, are mentioned in 1552, though not by name, as 'to be repaired and kept' and one of them appears under the name *Mermaid* in 1562 with two new companions, the *Speedwell* and *Tryright*, built in 1559. Before 1565 the *Mermaid* had been replaced by the *Eleanor*, another French prize, rebuilt in 1584 as the *Bonavolia*. By the end of Elizabeth's reign these three ships had disappeared and their places had been taken by four new galleys built in 1601-2, the *Superlativa*, *Advantagia*, *Gallarita* and *Volatillia*. These were still in existence in 1618, but were then described as 'decayed and unserviceable.'

As the last true galleys to be built in England these four vessels deserve a little consideration, but unfortunately there is hardly anything to consider; all we know of them is that they were rowed by about 240 men each. A keel-length of about 100 ft and 30 oars a side with four men on each is a mere guess, but may not be far

[1] Oppenheim, *The Administration of the Royal Navy*, p. 12.

84

from the truth; while the *Bonavolia* with 150 rowers may have had 25 oars a side. The rig was probably lateen.

Northern galleys descended from the Viking long-ships had been extinct for almost 300 years; balingers, of which we know next to nothing, for nearly as long. Now southern-type galleys had gone the same way and gunboats, as important units in a fleet, were still a long way in the future. In the meantime, roughly between 1600 and 1800, oars in the north, or at least in England, played little part save as auxiliaries to sails in various hybrid craft which, as time went on, lost all resemblance to one ancestor and became practically indistinguishable from normal sailing men-of-war.

The story is for the most part one of unrealised projects known only from draughts or models. First comes a remarkable ship shown in a coloured draught in the National Maritime Museum (Plate 18A). This is so similar in style and in the general appearance of the ship to another believed by Laughton, probably rightly, to represent the *Phoenix* of 1613[1] that one would put it also well back in the 17th century, were it not for the presence in the decoration of the letters C.R. As it is, its date cannot be before 1625, but is certainly very little later.

The dimensions indicated – keel 96 ft, beam 32 ft – are surprisingly large for a ship showing only 10 broadside ports; they are in fact those of contemporary ships of 32–34 guns. There are 16 oars a side, 5 ft apart, and a sectional drawing shows that these were to be worked by four men each.

Although the actual ship was never built, it is interesting to consider the probable origin of the drawing. If Laughton was right in identifying the similar draught as that of the *Phoenix* and Salisbury right in believing that the fragmentary drawing found on the back of the parchment can only represent some stage in the design of the *Prince Royal*,[2] we have a twofold association with Phineas Pett and he tells us in his autobiography that he spent the last part of the year 1625 'about building of small ships and presenting plats of them, both to the King and Commissioners of the Navy, to very little purpose — —.' It seems more than likely that this is one of the plats in question.

Other proposals for 'nimble and forcible' ships to meet the Dunkirkers were made about this time, but the 10 *Lion's Whelps* of 1627, though designed with that purpose in view, were much smaller and of old-fashioned proportions which made them far from nimble. We know little more than their dimensions and armament; they

---

[1] *Old Ship Figureheads and Sterns*, p. 262 and Plate 12.
[2] See *The Mariner's Mirror*, 1961, p. 170.

were intended 'to row as well as sail,' measured 62 ft on the keel with a beam of 25 ft and carried 12 guns of four different sizes from 32-prs to 6-prs. The French *Dragons* of slightly later date were a little larger and had 16 guns; while the fact that they had crews of 120 men as against 70 suggests that they had more oars or employed more men on each. The *Whelps* were a failure; they were too heavily armed to be seaworthy and too slow under either sail or oars to have any chance of overhauling the light frigates of Dunkirk, the task for which they had been built.

The word frigate or something very similar can be found in all European languages and its meaning has been the same everywhere at any given date, but has changed from century to century. Originally, as a southern word, it denoted the smallest member of the galley family, used mainly as a despatch-boat or tender. Towards the end of the 16th century, the Spaniards applied it to the light sailing ships employed between their American possessions and the home country and from these it spread to cover the small, fast and handy ships used by the semi-piratical privateers of Dunkirk and Ostend. Then, in the 1640's, ships of somewhat similar design began to appear in England to cope with these troublesome enemies.

What ship should be called the first English frigate is still a matter of dispute, but it can be said with certainty that the first ships of the new type built as public men-of-war as opposed to privateers were the *Nonsuch*, *Adventure* and *Assurance* of 1646 and it is just these three ships which we find mentioned in an account of a chase in 1651 as 'being fitted with oar-ports between the guns.' At first these Commonwealth frigates[1] had a complete tier of guns on the lower deck, but none above them in the waist. Soon, however, the need to face enemies heavier than the Dunkirkers led to the addition of more guns and made them into complete two-deckers.

This stage in the story of the frigate is illustrated by a model in the National Maritime Museum (No. 1660–2), a small two-decker with a total of 48 broadside ports and with 18 oar-ports on either side disposed in pairs between the lower-deck guns (Plate 18B). This is probably a model of the *Nantwich* of 1654; certainly it represents a ship of the same class and about the same date. Two smaller ships of this period, the *Merlin* and *Martin*, sometimes had the word 'galley' added to their names and the proportions of the *Merlin*, more than four beams to the keel, show that she at least was built with speed under oars in mind. The *Drake* of the same date was even more extreme; her ratio of keel to beam was almost 4¾.

Very soon the name frigate was being applied to nearly all men-

---

[1] The name is not strictly accurate, but is used for convenience.

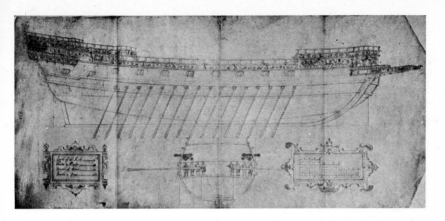

PLATE 18A. Draught of projected vessel, *c.* 1625. National Maritime Museum

PLATE 18B. Model of 40-gun frigate, *c.* 1655. National Maritime Museum.
(Author's photograph)

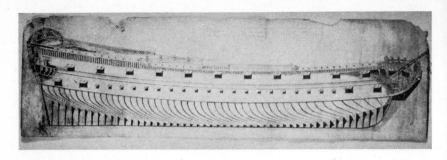

PLATE 19A. Drawing of the *Charles* galley, 1676. National Maritime Museum

PLATE 19B. Model of 20-gun ship, *c.* 1695. Now in Rogers' Collection, Annapolis (No. 14). Photograph taken before 'restoration'

PLATE 20A. Model of 32-gun ship, 1702. Pitt-Rivers Museum, Oxford

PLATE 20B. Model of 20-gun Sixth-Rate, *c.* 1720. Maidstone Museum

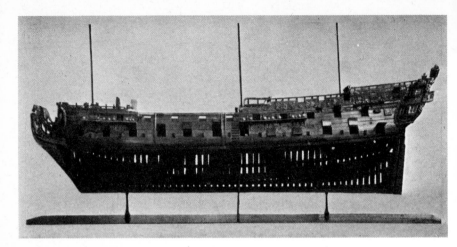

PLATE 21A. Model of 60-gun ship, *c.* 1730. National Maritime Museum.
(Author's photograph)

PLATE 21B. Swedish hemmema *Styrbjörn*, 1789. Contemporary model in
Sjöhistoriska Museum, Stockholm

of-war of modern design. Frigates were distinguished from ships not by size but by date, the line being drawn somewhere in the 1640s; even three-deckers were occasionally called frigates. Eventually the name came to denote ships of about 30–40 guns, some two-deckers, some not. It was not again used for a definite type of ship until the appearance of the so-called 'true frigates' about the middle of the 18th century.

In the meantime, English builders had made several attempts to produce a satisfactory blend of the sailing ship and the galley. The best known of these hybrids are the *Charles Galley* and *James Galley* both built in 1676, of which we have dimensions, plans, paintings and drawings (Plate 19A). Pepys tells us that their design was cribbed from that of French ships built at Toulon, but it is not clear what ships these were. At the same time there was in the Royal Navy a single real southern galley, built at Pisa in 1671 for service at Tangier. With the coming of the new galley-frigates she was given away as being an expense rather than an asset and the experiment was never repeated.

The two new ships resembled Henry VIII's galeasses in working their oars on the lower deck and having a full tier of guns above them, but had also two gun-ports on either side at each end of the lower deck beyond the 20 oars. In their descendants, the true frigates of Nelson's day, the lower deck carried no guns at all, though it was still called the gun-deck.

Except for the *Mary Galley*, of which not much is known,[1] the building of oared ships in England seems to have ceased for some 40 years, though models dating from the turn of the century show that the idea was not dead. First is a model now in America[2] of a ship with 20 ports on the upper deck, four on the quarter-deck and two, right aft on the lower deck, where there are also nine oar-ports on each side (Plate 19B). Its date can be fixed by the monogram 'W.R.' as 1694–1702. A remarkable feature of this model is that it shows dimensions so nearly fitting the 32-gun ships of the same period that one is tempted to try to find places for another eight guns. Certainly it has no resemblance to the normal single-decked 24-gun ship such as is shown by a well authenticated model of 1697.

Next is a model of 1702 in the same collection as this last, the Pitt-Rivers Museum at Oxford. This again is a two-decked ship, with 22 ports on the upper deck and six on the quarter-deck; while

[1] Built as a 34-gun ship she was rebuilt as a 40- in 1708 and then had the dimensions of that class of small 2-deckers.

[2] Annapolis, Rogers Collection, No. 14. The model has been very violently 'restored', but the 'W.R.' is original.

on the lower deck it has gun-ports in three groups, four forward, two amidships and four aft, with 24 oar-ports there as well (Plate 20B). The ship would have been too long and too narrow for any known ship and so definitely of galley type.

Among the designs prepared for ships of various classes in connection with the Establishment of 1719 there was one for a 30-gun ship with guns and oars arranged in much the same way. In this case the lower deck had on either side three gun-ports forward, one amidships and three aft, with the oars in two groups of five; there were 10 ports a side on the upper deck and two on the quarter-deck. No ships were actually built on this design, but it is worth recording as the final development in England of the type introduced by the *Charles Galley*. In France something of the sort cropped up again as late as 1785, though probably only as another unrealised project. A model in the Musée de Marine shows what would be a normal 32-gun frigate, if it were not for the presence of 20 oar-ports a side on the lower deck with four gun-ports, one forward, one amidships and two aft.[1] In its general design this model is almost a repetition of the English model of 1702.

The 20-gun ships of the English 1719 Establishment might be called throw-backs. Previous ships of their force had been single-decked, but these were structurally two-deckers with the lower deck given up entirely to the oars. Allowing for the many changes in details since 1546 they might be said to be copies of Henry VIII's galeass *Bull*; at the same time they must undoubtedly be considered the direct ancestors of the frigates of the second half of the century. Plate 20B shows one of these 20-gun ships.

Curiously enough, the 6th-Rates built under the later Establishments of 1733, 1741 and 1745 returned part of the way towards the design of the *Charles Galley*, since they all had a pair of gun-ports on either side at the after end of the lower deck, though only two guns were carried for the four ports. Not all were actually built with oar-ports, but all had these four gun-ports on the lower deck.

Then, with the *Lyme* and *Unicorn* of 1748, or perhaps some French ship of a few years earlier,[2] there arrived the 'true frigate,' in which the lower-deck guns disappeared for good. Not much need be said about oars in these ships, for though draughts and models sometimes show oar-ports between the guns both in frigates and in the smaller single-decked sloops until the 1790's, that is all; we never hear of their using these oars, if they carried them.

From the *Charles Galley* onwards all the ships or projects so far

---

[1] Illustrated in *Souvenirs de Marine*, Vol. 4, Plates 219–222.
[2] See *The Mariner's Mirror*, 1941, p. 160.

mentioned were two-deckers in the structural sense, but not in the sense of carrying two complete tiers of guns. There is, however, one model still to be considered in which we find a genuine 60-gun two-decker designed to use oars, a return to something very like the Commonwealth frigates in their later form, but on a larger scale. Unfortunately neither the nationality nor the date of this model has yet been determined with any approach to certainty. It is to be found in the National Maritime Museum (No. 1730–3) and shows a ship with ports on each broadside for 30 guns and 11 oars, these being placed between the lower-deck guns (Plate 21A). In the catalogue, for which I was responsible, it is described as 'perhaps Spanish, about 1730' and that is quite as far as it is safe to go at present. We can only say that it represents the largest square-rigged ship known to have been fitted to use oars since the days of Henry VIII's *Great Galley*. As such it has its importance in spite of the vagueness of our ideas as to its origin.

XI

Oared Men-of-War in the Baltic

Just as the galley was nearing the end of its useful life in the Mediterranean it and other oared craft began to take an important place in two of the Baltic navies, the Swedish and Russian. The last fleet-action in which Mediterranean galleys took part was that of Matapan in 1717; the first large galley action in the Baltic had been fought near Hangö in 1714. From then until Napoleonic times rowing vessels, not necessarily actual galleys, formed an essential part of both Swedish and Russian fleets.

The reason for this lay in the nature of the Finnish coastline, since it was Finland which the Russians were attacking and the Swedes defending throughout this period. All along the north side of the Gulf of Finland there runs a strip of rocks and islands which prevents sailing ships of any great size from approaching the mainland except at a few projecting headlands and at the same time provides a series of sheltered channels for small craft from Viborg in the east to the Aaland islands in the west. Without control of this coastal archipelago, the skärgaard, a sailing fleet, however strong, could do little towards co-operating with an army ashore; the necessary link could only be formed by a flotilla of rowing vessels.

Peter the Great was quick to recognise this, for as soon as he had brought the frontiers of Russia to the shores of the Baltic he began to build galleys in large numbers. Some of these, the larger, were actually so called, others were half galleys or *skampaveas*, but to their opponents and to the English officer who wrote an account of the ensuing campaigns[1] they were all galleys, though no doubt varying in size and fighting power.

Galleys more or less resembling those of the Mediterranean were not quite a novelty in northern waters, though they had only appeared in the last 50 years and that in very small numbers. There

[1] *The Russian Fleet under Peter the Great*, Navy Records Society, 1899.

had indeed been small craft so called in both Sweden and Norway as far back as the middle of the 16th century, but these had been of quite different type. Two built at Stavanger in 1618 are known to have been square-rigged three-masters with 30–34 oars, probably not unlike the English *Martin* and *Merlin* mentioned above. It was not until 1664, when Kort Adeler (or Curt Adelaer) had become Danish Admiral Lieutenant, that what may be called real galleys appeared in the north.[1]

Adeler, a Norwegian by birth, had served with distinction between 1645 and 1660 in one or more of the Dutch ships hired by Venice during the long Cretan war and had thus had full opportunity to form an estimate of a galley's usefulness. That estimate must evidently been favourable, since he at once arranged for a galley 'after the Turkish manner' to be built in Holland and reassembled at Bergen. It will be seen that this strange course of ordering a pattern galley from Dutch builders instead of Italian or French was repeated by Peter the Great 30 years later.

The *Friderich*, as this first Danish galley was called, measured 107 ft from stem to sternpost and 16 ft in moulded beam.[2] Her rig consisted of the usual two lateens and she carried seven guns, three firing forward and two on either side; her number of oars was 34. An ivory model believed to represent her shows a more definite forecastle than was usual in her southern relatives and a smaller poop (Plate 22A). Five similar galleys were soon built in Denmark and three in Norway, but these were smaller. Wartime experience led to a return in 1684 to much the same dimensions as those of the *Friderich* and the galleys built in 1710–1716 were a good deal larger.[3]

The Swedes were extraordinarily slow in realising that well armed rowing vessels were an absolute necessity for the defence of such coasts as that of Finland and a great part of their own. They did instruct one of their builders, who was then in Holland, to get the plans of Adeler's galley and it is possible he succeeded, for

---

[1] Jal, *Archéologie Navale*, Vol. 1, p. 348, quotes a statement by Olaus Magnus that Gustavus I of Sweden had 'biremes, triremes and quadriremes built about 1540 by Venetians engaged at great expense,' but Zettersten, *Svenska Flottans Historia*, 1522–1634, p. 324, points out that there is no trace of this in Swedish records. Swedish galleys at this time were mainly built in Finland and were probably of purely northern type.

[2] Holck, *Cort Adeler*, Copenhagen, 1934, p. 120. The figures given for these galleys by the same writer in *Lists of Men-of-War*, 1650–1700, Part 3, Society for Nautical Research, 1936, differ somewhat. I have followed the earlier, more specialised work, converting from Danish fleet of 314 mm. to English of 305.

[3] Their dimensions are not recorded, but they had crews of from 167 to 203 men, whereas the Swedish *Ulysses*, whose length was 90 ft, was given only 130 men after her capture by the Danes in 1716.

Sheldon, an English shipwright, built a 'Turkske galej' at Gothenburg in 1665, but a similar attempt to crib the design of two Danish galleys built at Christiansand in 1684 led to nothing. It was not until the Russian threat became serious that any sort of programme of galley building was attempted, and then it was too late.

Peter the Great launched the first galleys of his new Baltic navy in 1704, but he had already had such vessels in his short-lived Black Sea fleet, or rather river Don flotilla. The first of these was built in Holland in 1695, taken down and shipped to Archangel, transported by barge and sledge to Moscow and used as the pattern for 22 others, the whole number being then reassembled on the upper Don for their journey of some 800 miles to the Black Sea.

A model of this first Russian galley, now in the Rijks Museum in Amsterdam (Plate 22B), shows that she was very like her Mediterranean contemporaries, but much smaller, having 16 oars a side as against their 25-30.[1] Except for an increase in the beam of the true hull and a corresponding reduction in the projection of the outrigger her design was purely southern. As had been the case with the galley built for Denmark 30 years before, Dutch builders had been content to copy what had been for many years a standard type.

No record of the dimensions of this galley or her Russian-built sisters has been preserved, but they can be found with fair certainty from the model as being 99 ft (English) from stem to sternpost with a beam of 22 ft outside the planking and 24½ ft extreme.[2]

The galleys built in 1697-8 were longer and narrower; most of them were about 140 ft long and 20 ft wide, the figures presumably referring to length from stem to sternpost and beam without the outriggers. One was much larger still with a length of 174 ft and a beam of 24 ft, well up to contemporary Mediterranean standard.[3] Her number of pairs of oars is not recorded, but can hardly have been less than 30.

---

[1] The model has 34 oars, but the galley was classed as one of 32 and was actually handled by 28.

[2] These figures are based on the assumption that the scale of the model is $\frac{1}{17.6}$ ($\frac{5}{8}$ in. to 1 ft of 11 in. Amsterdam measure). They give a relation between length and number of oars agreeing with that found in early Danish and Swedish examples. A scale of $\frac{1}{24}$ ($\frac{1}{2}$ in. to 1 ft) might seem more likely, but the resulting dimensions would be too great. Elagin, 'The Azov Period,' p. 31, gives figures for keel, waterline and over-all length obviously derived from the model on the same assumption, but makes the extreme beam 'about 30 ft.' My measurements were obtained from the Museum.

[3] See The Mariner's Mirror, 1956, p. 181, for Mediterranean practice at this date. The figures given there are probably in Swedish feet and about 3 per cent should be subtracted to bring them to English or Russian measure.

Later galleys of the Black Sea fleet were smaller again and had only 16 pairs of oars. Even the *Dnyepr*, in which Catherine the Great made a Royal progress from Kiev to the sea in 1785, was only 110 ft long and 18 ft wide (20½ ft over all). This galley and her sister the *Don* were noteworthy in that they returned to the bireme arrangement of some 2,000 years before as shown in the Victory pediment. They had their oars in pairs with thole-pins about 1 ft apart carried in chocks so shaped as to put the aftermost thole slightly higher than the foremost. There were 15 such pairs on either side, so that the total number of oars was 60. The thwarts were also unusual; instead of being continuous and sloped aft towards the centre line they were in two sections, the inner about 18 in. abaft the outer.[1]

As had been the case in the Black Sea, the new Baltic fleet contained one galley much larger than the rest, 176 ft long and 25 ft wide. Of the others those actually classed as galleys were about 120 ft long and 16 ft wide, while the first *skampaveas* measured 72 ft by 10 ft. How many oars any of these rowed is uncertain. According to Veselago[2] the *skampaveas* engaged at Hangö in 1714 had 36 oars, but elsewhere[3] he gives a smaller number, 16 banks, for the galleys built at the same time in spite of the fact that these were some 80 per cent longer and that later vessels of their length are credited with 20 or 22 banks. The *Dvina* built in 1721 (Plate 23A) had 25 banks, but in general 20 or 22 remained the rule.

The building of galleys in Sweden began in 1712, when 12 were laid down, and in spite of the loss of at least that number during the next few years the flotillas in Stockholm and on the west coast totalled 30 galleys and half galleys or brigantines at the beginning of 1719. One galley was 154 ft long, others 97 or 90 ft and some less, while the brigantines were about 60–70 ft. A draught of one of the 90-ft class, the *Ulysses* captured by the Danes in 1716, shows 30-oared galley of the usual Mediterranean type, but with at least a suggestion of a three-masted square rig. That something of the sort was considered is shown by a design for a very small half-galley or 'double shallop' in which alternative rigs are shown.[4]

By the time the war ended (1721) bitter experience had shown

---

[1] These details are taken from a Russian draught included in the Admiralty collection in the National Maritime Museum. Draughts of smaller Russian boats show the same arrangement of the oars.

[2] *'History of the Russian Fleet'*, p. 251. The letter to which he refers does not use the word 'skampaveas,' but merely 'those of smaller dimensions;' while the fact that it describes *half* galleys as having 72 oars makes its authority very doubtful.

[3] *'List of Russian Ships of War'*, p. 344.

[4] Both these draughts are reproduced in *Svenska Flottans Historia*, Vol. 2 (1943), p. 50.

how essential it was for Sweden to have a flotilla able to face that of Russia with some hope of success, but money was lacking and little could be done. A commission was indeed sent to study the galleys of the Mediterranean and a programme was made out for increasing the number of galleys from 24, as it then stood, to 70; but neither this nor a subsequent programme with the number reduced to 41 was carried out. When the next war began in 1741, there were only about 20 galleys available.

In the matter of size no attempt was made to reach Mediterranean standard. There, galleys were being built with 25–30 pairs of oars and 145–170 ft long, whereas the new Swedish galleys were to have had 15–21 pairs of oars and a maximum length of about 136 ft. Even in 1748–9, when a real attempt to form a galley-fleet was at last made, the ships built were of only 20–22 banks and from 127 to 137 ft long. Plate 23B shows one of these galleys, the last that were built in Sweden. Apparently local conditions were against large galleys, for those built in Russia were of much the same size. A few with 25 banks appeared soon after 1760, but the great majority had the same number of oars as their Swedish opponents, though slightly longer.[1] The few galleys built in Denmark at this time were smaller still.

Now came a drastic reorganisation of the Swedish inshore fleet; in 1756 it ceased to belong to the Navy and became a branch of the Army. As such it was to be brought up to a strength of 80 galleys, but as the result of experience gained in operations on the coast of Pommerania in 1759 the building of galleys was abandoned altogether and new types of rowing vessels were introduced, far more heavily armed and consequently far less mobile. These vessels, designed by Chapman, the outstanding naval architect of the 18th century, together with their Russian counterparts, provided the Baltic's tardy contribution to the long story of rowing men-of-war.

The names given to the first three new types to appear were taken from those of Finnish provinces, Turunmaa, Uudenmaa and Pohjanmaa. The original design for a turuma was for a vessel measuring 117 ft by 29 ft (moulded) with 16 pairs of oars and carrying 12-prs as her heavy guns; those actually built in 1770 measured 123 ft by 30 ft and carried 18-prs. They had 19 pairs of oars working in crutches on a narrow outrigger above the main-deck ports and had a cut-down three-masted square rig without topgallants (Plate 24A). All these new vessels were originally designed with lateen rig and some were actually so fitted at first,

---

[1] A number of Russian galleys were 'altered to the Swedish fashion' in 1789. I have no idea what this involved.

PLATE 22A. Danish galley *Friderich*, 1667. Rosenborg Museum, Copenhagen

PLATE 22B. First Russian galley, built at Amsterdam, 1697. Rijks Museum, Amsterdam

PLATE 23A. Russian galley *Dvina*, 1721. Central Naval Museum, Leningrad

PLATE 23B. Swedish galley, 1749. Sjöhistoriska Museum, Stockholm

PLATE 24A. Swedish turuma *Lodbrok*, 1771. Sjöhistoriska Museum, Stockholm

PLATE 24B. Swedish udema *Thorborg*, 1772. Sjöhistoriska Museum, Stockholm

PLATE 25A. Swedish pojama *Brynhilda*, 1776. Sjöhistoriska Museum, Stockholm

PLATE 25B. Swedish kanonjoll, 1778. Sjöhistoriska Museum, Stockholm

but square rig soon became the rule. The usual armament of a turuma consisted of 24 18-prs and 16 3-prs, but there were slight variations.

The udema was by far the most revolutionary in design and seems to have been the least successful. She carried her main armament in a narrow battery on the middle-line with traversing carriages allowing all these guns to be used on either broadside. Her 18 pairs of oars were worked on the same deck and so could not be used while the guns were in action. The rig was that of a polacca-bark without topgallants and the usual armament was nine 12-prs in the battery, two 18-prs forward and two 8-prs aft. The dimensions were 118 ft by 28 ft (Plate 24B).

A pojama had a pair of 24-prs at either end on traversing carriages which allowed them – with considerable difficulty – to be brought to bear on either broadside as well as ahead or astern; she had also 12 3-pr swivels. She measured 90 ft by 26 ft and had 16 pairs of oars and a rig like that of a bomb-ketch, but with the main-mast farther forward (Plate 25A). Very few of this class were built; their place was taken by the smaller 'kanonslupar' and 'kanonjollar' which will be described shortly.

Before doing this it will be as well to deal with the Russian 'opposite numbers' of the Swedish vessels already mentioned and with a fourth class which came into service during the war of 1788–90. This, the hemema (from the Finnish Hämmenmaa) was much larger than her predecessors and differed less from a normal deep-sea ship; she was in fact simply a shallow-draught frigate or sloop with oar-ports on the main deck. With a length of 142 ft and a beam of 35 ft she carried 24 36-prs and two 12-prs on a draught of 10 ft. The oars, 20 on either side, were worked through ports arranged in pairs between the guns; the rig was that of a frigate with topmasts and topgallants in one piece (Plate 21B). Two later ships built in 1809 had the same dimensions, but only half the number of oars. They carried 22 36-prs and 10 24-prs.[1]

It was not until the outbreak of war in 1788 that any move was made in Russia to produce vessels similar or equivalent to the new Swedish classes. Galley building had ceased in Sweden since 1749, but in Russia it went on for another 25 years and there were even a few built as late as 1796. These last Russian galleys were unusual in carrying a heavy gun aft firing over the rudder-head as well as three forward. They measured 127 ft by 21 ft and rowed 22 oars a

---

[1] Two illustrated articles on these Swedish types by Rear-Admiral J. Hägg appeared in *The Mariner's Mirror* in 1913.

side.[1] Half-galleys, or kaiks, built about 1770, had 11 pairs of oars and were 70 ft long.

'Rowing frigates', 'shebeks', 'half shebeks' and 'secret vessels' appeared in 1789 and 1790 in answer to the demands of active service. The first of these must have been very like the Swedish hemema, but smaller. They measured 130 ft by 32 ft with a draught of 11 ft and carried 38 guns. The shebek, a corruption of xebec, was derived from a southern type, but was near enough to a turuma to let Swedish ships of that class be called shebeks when in Russian hands. Eight of these were built and all were 120 ft long; four were 30 ft wide and drew less than 8½ ft, the others were 4 ft wider and drew 11½ ft, but strangely enough the smaller ships carried 50 guns and the larger only 32. No doubt the average weight of the 50 guns was less than that of the 32 and in general all these Russian ships seem to have carried guns lighter than those of their Swedish opponents. Some shebeks had a lateen on the foremast with square sails on the main and mizzen, others had exactly the rig of a turuma. Their number of oars was 40.

Half-shebeks were much smaller, only 76 ft by 19 ft. They were also called schooners, but were certainly not rigged as such. What rig they did carry is hard to say. One Russian authority describes Swedish pojamas as schooner-rigged and Russian half shebeks or schooners as having two masts with lug-sails;[2] but we know that a pojama was practically an old-fashioned square-rigged ketch and the only available representation of a Russian half shebek (a Swedish drawing) shows her with a lateen forward and a gaff-sail aft with a square topsail above it.[3] The guns were disposed as in a pojama, two forward and two aft, but were 18-prs instead of 24-prs.

The three 'secret vessels' are said to have been based on the design of a Swedish udema,[4] but they are credited with 44 guns and it is hard to see how such a ship could carry the 30 or more small guns needed to make up that number; a turuma seems a more likely pattern. They were 120 ft long and 28 ft wide and had 22 pairs of oars.

The Swedish hemema was not copied in Russia until 1808. Two ships of the kind were captured at Sveaborg in that year and may

---

[1] The plans of one of these 1796 galleys were reproduced by Paris in *Souvenirs de Marine*, Vol. 5, Plate 291. He took the scale as $\frac{1}{40}$, whereas it should be $\frac{1}{48}$ ($\frac{1}{4}$ in. to 1 ft). It is true that he describes the dimensions he gives as 'written on the Russian plans,' but this must have been done by someone who made the same mistake of thinking the Russian draughtsman would use the metric system. As the plans appear, half the size of the original, they are exactly on $\frac{1}{96}$.

[2] Golovatchev, '*Operations of the Russian Fleet*', 1788–90, Vol. 1, pp. 143, 161.

[3] Reproduced in *Svenska Flottans Historia*, Vol. 2, p. 379.

[4] Golovatchev, p. 161.

have provided the pattern, though the first Russian copy was afloat only two months later. In any case the Russians were very like the original, their dimensions being 143¾ ft by 35½ ft. They had 32 guns, as had the two Swedish ships built at the same time; the number of oars is not recorded. One solitary representative of this class was launched as late as 1823.

All the new types so far described were limited in numbers built, in geographical distribution and in length of useful life, but the position as regards the two smaller classes was very different. 'Gun-sloops' and 'gun-yawls'[1] were produced in hundreds, were used from the Gulf of Finland to the west coast of Norway and remained in use until oars were replaced by steam.

Although, as has been said, Russia went on building galleys long after Sweden had ceased to do so, it was in Russia that we first find an attempt made to produce a smaller type of well armed rowing vessel for use in narrow waters. The first Russian double-sloop was launched in 1764 and others of the same class were built until 1776. They were 70 ft long and 14 ft wide with 10 pairs of oars and eight guns, but how many of these were more than swivels and how they were disposed is uncertain. In any case the design became obsolete on the appearance in Sweden soon after 1775 of the gunboats which played so important a part in the wars of 1788–90 and 1807–14.

These were of two kinds, both introduced by Chapman. The first, the gun-sloop, had a heavy gun at each end on a carriage which could be slid down towards the keel for stability under sail. At first the guns were an 18-pr and a 12-pr, but by 1789 both were 24-prs; there were also four 3-pr swivels. Dimensions grew from 62 ft by 13½ ft to 66½ ft by 14½ ft. There were 14 or 15 pairs of oars and two masts carrying lateen sails.

The gun-yawl carried a single heavy gun aft, usually a 24-pr. This was mounted in a fixed carriage, so that the recoil of the gun drove the whole boat forward at each discharge and made it necessary to use the oars to get back into position. She was double ended under water and had her decked stern cut down to the waterline or very near it, to let the gun be placed more nearly amidships and still leave an unobstructed field of fire aft. This double-endedness made it almost as easy to row stern first as bow first and did away with the need to turn round within range of

---

[1] These two names represent the Swedish *kanonslupar* and *kanonjollar* or the Danish *kanonchalupper* and *kanonjoller*. 'Shallop' and 'jolly (boat)' might be better, since both 'sloop' and 'yawl' give an unjustified suggestion of rig. The two classes could be included under the term 'gunboats' and that name, *kanonerskia lodki*, was used in Russia for all these small craft.

the enemy. Her dimensions were 41 ft by 10 ft and she had two masts with standing lugs (Plate 25B).

As had been the case with the larger vessels, Russian imitations of these Swedish gunboats appeared first in 1788. All were called simply gunboats, but their dimensions divided them into two groups and it is more than likely that these corresponded roughly to the Swedish sloops and yawls.

The larger boats were from 62 to 68 ft long and 14 or 15 ft wide. They had 14 or 15 pairs of oars and for the most part carried two heavy guns, though some had only one. In 1809 and 1812 larger boats were built, 81 ft by 17 ft with two or three guns, but after that there was a return to the old dimensions. The last Russian rowing gunboats were built as late as 1854 and had 20 pairs of oars and two guns; they measured about 74 ft by 17 ft. Some of these were engaged by British ships off Aabo (Turku) in August of that year and this was probably the last occasion on which rowing vessels fired their guns in action.

Comparatively few of the Russian gunboats belonged to the yawl class. A few boats measuring 45 ft by 14 ft with one gun and nine pairs of oars were built in 1788 and these probably resembled the Swedish boats of similar size, but a few others about 53 ft long are more likely to have been reduced gun-sloops; they carried two guns and it is hard to see how this could have been the case in anything of the yawl design.

Denmark, which in those days meant also Norway, was the last of the Baltic countries to take to these heavily armed small craft and may be said to have made the fullest use of them. In the Anglo-Danish war of 1807–14 gunboats, in sufficient numbers and in suitable weather, proved themselves able to engage much larger sea-going ships, even two-deckers, with fair hope of success.

According to a modern Swedish writer, Russia obtained plans or at least full details of the new Swedish vessels in 1787 by way of Denmark.[1] This can hardly be true as regards the gunboats, because it was found necessary to send a Danish shipbuilder to Sweden in 1791 to try to find out how they were built and it was not until 1805 that information given by a former Swedish officer allowed their design to be reproduced in Denmark.[2]

The last Danish galleys had been launched in 1764–7 and had actually been slightly smaller than their predecessor of 100 years before. They were 98 ft long and 17¾ ft wide and had 16 pairs of oars; their armament consisted of one 12-pr, two 3-prs and 12

[1] Munthe, *Flottan och Ryska Kriget*, Vol. 4, p. 62.
[2] Schultz, *Den Danske Marine*, 1814–1848, pp. 94 and 97.

swivels. In 1786 an attempt was made to find a satisfactory substitute in the *skiaerbaad* (skerry-boat), much shorter, 66 ft by 17½ ft, but with the same number of oars; these boats had two 18-prs foward and 6 small howitzers.

The short campaign on the west coast of Sweden in 1788 showed the superiority of the new Swedish gunboats and led to the effort already mentioned to obtain access to their plans. The first attempted copies were based on incomplete information and proved unsatisfactory, but from 1805 onwards Danish gun-sloops were almost exact duplicates of the Swedish and equally efficient. The only noteworthy difference lay in rig, where the Danes had two lugs with a foresail and a small jigger in place of the Swedes' two lateens.

Plans of the Swedish *kanonjollar* were obtained at the same time and were also followed very closely. An apparent difference in length, 37½ ft in the Danish boats as against 41 ft in the Swedish, may possibly be due to different methods of measuring, though the figures for the gun-sloops of the two countries are almost identical. The rig of Danish yawls was the same as that of the sloops.

These two types of small craft served with distinction throughout the war of 1808–14 and there was no need to modify them. It was not until 1831 that new designs were produced to accommodate guns firing 60-lb shells. The new sloops carried one 60-pr shell gun forward, one ordinary 24-pr aft and four 4-pr howitzers; the yawls had the same shell-gun aft and two 4-pr. Dimensions were 67¼ ft by 15 ft for the sloops, a very small increase, and 50½ ft by 10¼ ft for the yawls. The first class was rigged with two lugs and a jigger, the second with two spritsails. Oars were 15 and nine pairs respectively.

The final development of the gun-sloop at the western end of the Baltic came in 1848, when 12 of these were built at Kiel for the revolting dependencies of Schleswig-Holstein. These were all handed over to the Danish navy in 1852. Their designer had worked in the Copenhagen dockyard and produced vessels very like the Danish, but rather heavier in construction and rig. In them there was a 60-pr shell-gun at either end, but the foremost could no longer be lowered when not in use. They measured 66¼ ft by 14½ ft, almost exactly the same as the Swedish vessels of 60 years before. If it had not been for the coming of steam, the Baltic gunboat might well have become as nearly a standardised type as the Mediterranean galley had been in her day.

Index